BRITAIN'S DECLINING SECONDARY RAILWAYS
THROUGH THE 1960s

~m~ **THE BLAKE PATERSON COLLECTION** ~m~

BRITAIN'S DECLINING SECONDARY RAILWAYS

THROUGH THE 1960s

THE BLAKE PATERSON COLLECTION

Kevin McCormack and Martin Jenkins

PEN & SWORD
TRANSPORT

First published in Great Britain in 2016 by
Pen & Sword Transport
An imprint of Pen & Sword Books Ltd
47 Church Street
Barnsley
South Yorkshire
S70 2AS

ISBN 978 1 47386 0 292

Typeset by Pen & Sword Books Ltd

Printed and bound by Imago Publishing Limited

Pen & Sword Books Ltd incorporates the imprints of Pen & Sword Archaeology, Atlas, Aviation, Battleground, Discovery, Family History, History, Maritime, Military, Naval, Politics, Railways, Select, Social History, Transport, True Crime, and Claymore Press, Frontline Books, Leo Cooper, Praetorian Press, Remember When, Seaforth Publishing and Wharncliffe.

For a complete list of Pen & Sword titles please contact
Pen & Sword Books Limited
47 Church Street, Barnsley, South Yorkshire, S70 2AS, England
E-mail: enquiries@pen-and-sword.co.uk
Website: www.pen-and-sword.co.uk

Front cover: Brighton-based Ivatt 2-6-2T, No.41302 stands at Bramley & Wonersh station on a Guildford-Horsham working on 18 January 1964. The line, which was nineteen miles long, closed on 14 June 1965, just under four months short of its centenary. All the railway structures at Bramley, apart from the platforms, were quickly demolished but, to improve the Downs Link footpath and bridleway that now occupies the trackbed, some features have since been replicated including the up platform shelter (behind the signal box) and the level crossing gates. One of the reinstated enamel station nameboards had been used as a shelf in a Worthing greenhouse! A fragment of the main station building survives because it contains a Royal Mail post box.

Title page: A shaft of sunlight catches a trio of railway workers at Woodford Halse shed in Northamptonshire on 19 January 1963. The depot opened due to the construction of the London extension of the Great Central Railway and, combined with a marshalling yard and railway station (called Woodford and Hinton until 1948), turned a small village into a minor railway town (it has now returned to being a village). The shed closed to steam on 14 July 1965 and Great Central services in the area were withdrawn on 5 January 1966. Woodford Halse was primarily a freight shed, as evidenced by the locomotives in the background that are mainly Standards. However, the depot had a small allocation of engines for local passenger trains, notably the Woodford-Banbury shuttles latterly hauled by Fairburn 2-6-4Ts, the final such service operating on 13 June 1964.

Rear cover: The date is 25 January 1964 and a Cravens two-car diesel multiple unit (DMU) is at the once busy Cairnie Junction station on the erstwhile Great North of Scotland Railway, which closed to passengers on 6 May 1968. Until the 'Beeching Axe' was wielded, there were three routes to Elgin from Cairnie Junction: an inland route via Craigellachie and a coastal route via Buckie, both now closed, leaving the mainline from Aberdeen to Inverness via Keith and Elgin as the only one remaining. Today's single track, previously doubled, runs through the middle of the island platform seen here so passengers now would be unaware that a junction station ever existed at this spot.

PREFACE

Following a few early spasmodic closures, a decrepit railway emerged from another war, only to be nationalised in 1948. Line closures began in earnest starting with the hopelessly uneconomic, as car ownership took hold. By 1960 panic set in about rail's viability with the urgent appointment of Dr Richard Beeching as the railway's new 'emperor'! His March 1963 'report' purely sped up what was already happening by listing a further 2,363 stations to close, 266 services to be withdrawn and the 'modification' of 71 others. Beeching formalised an ongoing existing situation and I had to be one step in front of the Doctor by recording a fast disappearing age.

Flanged wheels guided by rails along a predetermined route had fascinated me from an early age. Visits to my grandparents in Winchelsea, East Sussex, introduced me to South Eastern H Class 0-4-4T locomotives on push/pull workings to Hastings, and afternoon tea in the Pullman on an electric to Lewes brought a touch of elegance. This was followed by steam via Sheffield Park, before the illustrious Miss Bessemer had saved the Bluebell Railway's immediate closure by invoking an Act of Parliament, which was the highlight of the trip to East Grinstead, and then on to my Surrey home in Woldingham, giving another dose of steam.

From my Berkshire school, aged sixteen, I wrote to British Railways (BR) for possible employment. The letter was forwarded to the Western Region, though my actual home was on the Southern. So I joined the 'brown region' at Paddington in 1960 rather than the 'green' as a quirk of fate! Some senior staff still wore wing collars, most express trains were still painted chocolate and cream, so long as they were part of a 'named train', and varied stationmasters appearing for meetings delighted the 'Guv'nors' by wearing their Great Western pill box hats, albeit twelve years after nationalisation!

The District office saw me examining guards'

journals, which recorded each individual train journey. My eye caught interest in various steam-worked rural branch lines, which carried few, if any, passengers, and that's how it all started. I became mesmerised being chauffeured by steam through bucolic countryside with a guard and occasional passenger to keep me company in a world of forgotten ecstasy. How long could this bygone age of travel last? The camera clicked, and I soon had a wish list of lines to visit.

I took lodgings in West London where my landlady 'only took Great Western boys' in the mistaken belief that GW boys were a cut above the rest! Nevertheless 'foreign' inmates were carefully smuggled in! Alternate weekends were 'kicking out weekends', whereby one had to vacate the digs and lodge elsewhere. This was a marvellous incentive to go travelling. But with line closures speeding up under Beeching, it would have been pointless going in the wrong direction if one was going to get abysmal weather. People have commented that my pictures are always in the sun, but this was not luck. My strong rule was no sun, no picture, but I now regret taking few record shots. Time was against me. On a Friday morning I would listen to the countrywide weather outlook and then examine newspaper weather maps. After work I rechecked the radio weather forecast, by which time I had a good idea of what was happening. My final decision was taken minutes later, when one could actually speak to a person in the Met. Office about the possible location of blue skies. So off I went with my duffel bag and toothbrush, bought a ticket and took a chance often 'on the cushions' overnight! Yes, it worked most of the time, but that was for Saturdays; but on Sundays steam and branch lines had usually vanished, which accounts for my having tramped every sleeper during every season in the Isle of Wight where BR maintained its daily steam 'museum' service that seemed to go on forever!

Today, with more people travelling by train than ever, it's easy to jest that today's privatised railway is costing the earth to run, but Dr Beeching did not forecast what might happen after 1970 in the middle of warring politicians, each of whom had starved the railway of any real investment. He might now be pleasantly surprised!

And what did I achieve 4,500 pictures later, taken over a span of ten years? I enjoyed the delights of a railway with its dedicated staff that was forever Britain, as steam trains and branch lines raced one another to vanish into oblivion.

What happened next was I ventured over to France where a cull of secondary lines was about to happen. Schoolboy French announced 'Je suis venu d'Angleterre especialment pour visiter votre reseau curieuse!' which meant 'I have come over specially from England to visit your quaint railway!' This opened all the doors and my rural railway addiction started all over again … but that's another story!

My photographic mentors were Cam Camwell, who showed the importance of good three quarter front station views as a record, and Colin Gifford's dramatic 1965 tome *Decline of Steam* did the opposite in introducing the surreal in the form of a new dimension into atmosphere, people and the unconscious thought of the unusual.

Blake Paterson

AUTHORS' NOTE

This book, focusing exclusively on the photographs of Blake Paterson, has been compiled by railway enthusiasts Kevin McCormack and Martin Jenkins. Both are well-known transport authors and are also directors of Online Transport Archive, a registered charity that preserves collections of transport photographs and cine film, making these available for bona fide authors and film makers.

An attempt has been made to arrange the images in this book on a rough geographical basis, starting in the West Country and proceeding northwards, reaching Scotland and finally Ireland, including the Republic, albeit not part of 'Britain'. Blake was not following trains by car. He was travelling on them and without the friendliness of the railway guards and drivers who held trains until he had taken his photographs and often posed for the camera, Blake's evocative and hitherto unpublished work featured in this album would not have been achieved to the same degree.

Blake visited Cornwall on 28 May 1966 to record trains on the former Bodmin & Wadebridge Railway built in 1834 and a pioneer user of steam traction. The line was acquired by the London & South Western Railway (LSWR) in 1847 and was connected to the Great Western Railway (GWR) line to Bodmin for Bodmin Road in 1888 and extended westwards to Padstow in 1899. Following nationalisation of the railways in 1948, the former LSWR terminus at Bodmin was renamed Bodmin North and the ex-GWR terminus became Bodmin General. This view shows Nanstallon Halt, four miles east of Wadebridge looking towards Bodmin, and depicts a Western Region (WR) single-car diesel unit. The halt was opened by the LSWR on 2 July 1906 and later acquired a GWR 'Pagoda' shelter. The line closed to passengers on 30 January 1967.

In an unsuccessful attempt to make the Wadebridge-Bodmin services more sustainable two exchange platforms were installed at Boscarne Junction so that passengers from Bodmin North and Dunmere Halt could transfer to Bodmin General to Wadebridge trains. The Bodmin North shuttle, journey time five minutes, was introduced from 14 June 1964 and was operated by two railbuses, Nos.W79977 and W79978, belonging to a batch of five built by AC Cars of Thames Ditton with AEC engines. These had operated on the Tetbury and Cirencester branches from Kemble in Gloucestershire from 2 February 1959 until these lines closed on 4 April 1964. When the Bodmin shuttles were withdrawn on 30 January 1967, both railbuses were transferred to the Scottish Region. On his 28 May 1966 visit, Blake photographed one of these railbuses at Dunmere Halt, close to Dunmere Junction (think Wenfordbridge and Beattie tanks!). The halt displays its LSWR origins with the use of concrete posts but, like Nanstallon Halt, it later acquired a GWR Pagoda hut. The heritage Bodmin & Wenford Railway has reopened the line from Bodmin Parkway (formerly Bodmin Road) to Boscarne Junction via Bodmin General. Nanstallon and Dunmere halts are still in situ, improving the Camel Trail multi-purpose pathway, though you won't see any humpback animals! Camel is the name of the local river and valley.

Trains from Bodmin reached Padstow via Wadebridge, which was also the junction with the North Cornwall Railway from Halwill in Devon via Launceston and Camelford. This line, operated by the LSWR from the outset, was built in stages between 1886 and 1899 and closed on 3 October 1966, four months before the Wadebridge-Padstow line from Bodmin. Camelford station, towards the western end of the Halwill line, optimistically infers proximity to Boscastle and Tintagel but was nowhere near anywhere, not even Camelford town! One of Blake's interests was to record aspects of the vanishing infrastructure and on 28 May 1966 the station looks well past its prime.

Another station photographed on 28 May 1966 was Tresmeer, the second station east of Camelford. Opened on 28 July 1892 it was located near the delightfully named hamlet of Splatt, not to be confused with Splott that is a district of Cardiff.

Still proceeding eastwards, the station between Tresmeer and Launceston was Egloskerry, which on 28 May 1966 was typically deserted, apart from railway staff, one of whom, on the opposite platform, may be the signalman going to the hand-operated level crossing gates. The Halwill-Padstow line was never well patronised but it reflected the LSWR's desperation to reach Cornwall to challenge the GWR's monopoly in that county and to connect with its own Bodmin-Wadebridge-Padstow line. Latterly there were just four through trains in each direction on weekdays plus a morning run from Launceston to Hallwill and a return working in the evening. The narrow gauge Launceston Steam Railway now operates along 2½ miles of the North Cornwall Railway from Launceston to Newmills and hopes to extend to Egloskerry. The station houses at Camelford, Tresmeer and Egloskerry survive as private residences.

Further up the North Cornwall coast from Padstow is the seaside town of Bude, which was the terminus of a branch from Okehampton in Devon, diverging from the Padstow via Camelford line near Halwill Junction. Initially the LSWR built the line only as far as Holsworthy, opening the station in 1879, and provided a bus service to Stratton and Bude. The residents of those habitations pressed the LSWR to extend the railway, which they did nineteen years later, but decided on a more direct and less costly route avoiding Stratton, which, at the time, had a larger population than Bude. On 1 June 1963 Standard Class 4 2-6-4, No.80064 stands ready to leave Bude for Okehampton on one of eight weekday departures. Now no trace remains of the station, the railway land being covered by houses with an address of Bulleid Way. This commemorates the designer of West Country Pacific No.34006 *Bude*, the naming ceremony having taken place at Bude station on 1 November 1945. However, it is doubtful whether many residents on the estate know the significance of their road name, but at least they have been spared the more prosaic Beeching Close!

The Bude branch was transferred from the Southern Region (SR) to the WR on 1 January 1963 and, to save money, staff numbers were reduced and diesel units introduced from September 1964. The only intermediate station on the Holsworthy-Bude extension was Whitstone & Bridgerule and a single-car 'bubble' car unit is seen there on 28 May 1966 heading for Bude. Although Whitstone is in Cornwall and Bridgerule is in Devon, any county rivalries were disregarded in the context of this 'joint' station that stood just inside Devon and opened on 1 November 1898. The main station building, with its canopy intact, is now a private house and although the trackbed has been filled in, the platform edges are visible. Sadly, the two original LSWR enamel station signs on each platform, which surprisingly were still in place when passenger services were withdrawn, have been removed. The one pictured here on 1 June 1963 was located on the Bude platform opposite the main building and close to the road bridge.

After Holsworthy, travelling east, the next station on the Bude branch was Dunsland Cross, where the station nameboard invited passengers to alight for Shebbear College. The station opened on 20 January 1879 when the terminus of the Bude line was Holsworthy. The branch was single track with passing loops at the stations, hence the second platform. Once, long cattle trains had used this line as well as a portion of the 'Atlantic Coast Express' that ran on summer Saturdays until September 1964 but, by the time of Blake's visit on 28 May 1966, only local services operated and Dunsland Cross station was showing signs of neglect, including the partial collapse of a section of platform. The main station building survives as a bungalow.

Making his way east towards Okehampton on 28 May 1966, Blake alighted at Maddaford Moor Halt for Thorndon Cross. There he recorded passengers using the line, something which occurred all too infrequently, and which inevitably made the branch a target for the Beeching Axe. This primitive station was something of an afterthought as it did not open until 26 July 1926, forty-seven years after the line to Holsworthy was built. The sign on the extreme left attached to the 'station building' reads 'Waiting Shed', which is an apt description of the structure!

Three lines bifurcated at Halwill, as stated on the running-in board photographed on 28 May 1966. These were the LSWR's Bude Branch, the North Cornwall Railway to Launceston, later extended to Padstow, and the North Devon & Cornwall Light Railway to Torrington. The station closed to passengers on 3 October 1966 and the site has been redeveloped for housing, which includes a road inevitably called Beeching Close.

This scene at Halwill was taken on an earlier visit on 1 June 1963 when it was well endowed with signals. The train has a goods van in the middle, indicating it is formed of two portions, which would have originated from Padstow and Bude. The Bude section has arrived first, the locomotive subsequently running round its train and hauling the coaches on to the Bude branch until the Padstow section arrived. The Bude engine would then propel the coaches onto the back of the train for the onward journey, probably to Exeter Central. Judging by the empty Post Office trolley being pushed over the crossing, the combined train has probably been loaded with parcels. It is hauled by Maunsell Class N 2-6-0, No.31874, one of eighty built, and the sole representative of the class to have the good fortune to end up at Woodhams scrapyard at Barry. Consequently it is the only one preserved, its latest home being on the Swanage Railway.

One of the least profitable passenger lines in the country was that from Torrington to Halwill Junction, which was opened by the North Devon & Cornwall Junction Light Railway as late as 1925. This was the last standard gauge line built in North Devon and was constructed in part on the trackbed of a 3ft gauge industrial line dating from the 1880s. Latterly, the weekday service comprised a couple of through trains in each direction together with two early morning and one late afternoon part way journeys. Travelling from north to south on the 8.52am from Torrington, Blake photographed all the stations and halts during his visit on 3 June 1963, including Watergate Halt some 1¾ miles from Torrington. Here he jumped down from the carriage, crossed the road and clambered over a gate into a field to take this remarkable view of a stationary train 'in the middle of nowhere'.

Just under three miles further on from Watergate Halt was Yarde Halt where the spartan buildings typified the light railway's frugal infrastructure. This view was obtained by venturing across the ungated road crossing. The loco was an Ivatt Class 2 2-6-2T, No.41216 of Barnstaple motive power depot (mpd). Note the clay workers' cottages on the left.

Among other stations photographed on 3 June 1963 was Meeth Halt. This charming scene epitomises the bucolic nature of this isolated line. The lax schedule resulted in an average speed of little more than 15mph with the 20½ mile journey taking a very leisurely one hour and twenty-five minutes, which was meant to include any time for shunting en route. It also gave ample time for photography. On this occasion, Blake was told by the sympathetic guard, who was busy cooking his breakfast, 'Take your pictures and when you're ready go tell the driver' – an open invitation that couldn't be refused. On other occasions, enthusiasts were invited onto the loco and allowed to take charge of the regulator.

Hatherleigh was reached at 9.48am – a journey time of fifty-six minutes for under thirteen miles. Here there was a passing loop and goods yard. With extremely light passenger loadings, revenue was mostly derived from the bulk movement of heavy ball clay and bricks. As a result, some trains were mixed passenger and goods but, on this occasion, No.41216 was in charge of a single Bulleid composite coach. Following withdrawal of the passenger service on 1 March 1965, clay workings continued on the Torrington-Meeth section until 1982.

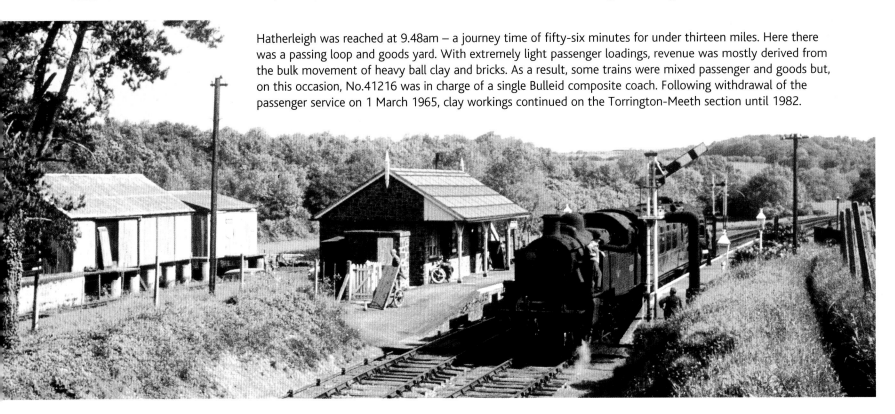

As this line had only recently been taken over by the Western Region, the driver has a brown WR badge on his cap. This single track light railway featured many twists, turns, sharp bends and ungated crossings, each of which was approached by a blast on the whistle. It is surprising the limited passenger service survived so long. Although always operated by the Southern Railway in pre-nationalisation days, this was one of a number of Colonel Stephens light railways that remained independent until the creation of BR in 1948.

The day before covering the Torrington-Halwill line, Blake took this evocative view. It shows another Ivatt 2-6-2T, No.41283 leaving Instow with a train for Bideford and Torrington composed of BR Mark I stock and a WR Syphon G van, possibly carrying milk churns. This line from Barnstaple, which initially terminated at Fremington (originally a horse-drawn tramway), was extended to Bideford in 1855 and onwards to Torrington in 1872. The relatively frequent passenger service over this 14¼ mile line stopped on 2 October 1965 but freight services continued over part of it until 1982. As late as September 1964, on summer Saturdays a single through coach had operated from Waterloo to Torrington as part of the 'Atlantic Coast Express'. A preservation society was set up with a view to purchasing the line but couldn't raise sufficient funds and the rails were lifted in 1985. The trackbed has become part of the Tarka Trail and the former LSWR signal box at Instow, which was the first example of this type of structure to receive Grade II listing, has been restored and is managed by the Bideford Railway Heritage Centre, based at the former Bideford station site. As well as controlling train movements at the station and adjoining goods yard, the signalman at Instow signal box was also responsible for the adjacent level crossing. Both are out of view in this picture, being situated behind the station building, which now belongs to the North Devon Yacht Club.

This is Portsmouth Arms on the former North Devon Railway, which opened between Crediton and Barnstaple in 1854 and was absorbed into the LSWR the following year. The station was named after the local public house, the Portsmouth Arms, which was itself named after the local landowner, the Earl of Portsmouth, through whose estate the railway passed and who demanded the right to stop trains whenever he wanted. Portsmouth Arms is a hamlet containing four dwellings, a sawmill, a farm, a station cottage, the inn and ex-SECR Kitchen First Pullman carriage No.136 *Formosa*, built in 1921 and undergoing restoration on a short length of track beside the station. Remarkably the station, which now consists of the ubiquitous bus shelter, is still open as a request stop and served by three trains a day in each direction between Exeter and Barnstaple on a community railway marketed as the 'Tarka Line'. The section of line between Copplestone and Umberleigh through Portsmouth Arms was never doubled, but, as seen here on 5 July 1964, Portsmouth Arms had a passing loop that remained in use until 1966.

The last station on the 'Tarka Line' before Barnstaple is Chapelton that, like Portsmouth Arms, is a request stop and is served by five trains a day. Opened in 1857 as Chapeltown, it closed as early as 1860 but reopened as Chapelton in 1875 in the form seen here, with a large gabled station house that is visible behind the train. The line is now singled, with only the down platform used today. The station house has become a private residence and part of the up platform has been retained. Blake was fortunate to capture this resplendent Bulleid West Country Light Pacific, *Seaton*, during his visit on 2 June 1963. Built at Brighton Works in 1945, No.34020 was transferred in May 1962 from Nine Elms to Exmouth Junction mpd where it was based when working this Barnstaple-Exeter duty. It was withdrawn in September 1964. A total of 110 West Country/Battle of Britain 'Pacifics' were built and twenty escaped the scrapman's torch, but sadly not 34020.

An alternative route to Barnstaple, this time from Taunton rather than Exeter, was built by the Devon & Somerset Railway and opened between 1871 and 1873. Initially operated by the Bristol & Exeter Railway (B&ER) and later by the GWR, this forty-three mile branch traversed undulating rural terrain that involved several viaducts and steep gradients. The latter needed fairly powerful locomotives and in the post-war era motive power was normally provided by Churchward/Collett 2-6-0 tender engines, represented here on 4 July 1964 at Bishop's Nympton and Molland by No.6345, which is heading one of the services between Taunton and Barnstaple, some of which had through carriages for Torrington. This station opened as Molland on 1 November 1873 but, since it was located between Bishop's Nympton and Molland, the name was altered in 1876 to recognise both villages. Later in 1964 a slimmed-down service worked by DMUs was introduced but failed to save this attractive line, with the last passenger train running on 1 October 1966. The main station building (behind the tall lamppost) is now a private residence. The once extensive movement of milk and cattle had long since transferred to the road.

The 19½ mile Exe Valley line, linking the Taunton to Barnstaple branch at Dulverton with the West of England main line at Exeter, was built by two companies, each reaching Tiverton separately. The section north of Tiverton opened on 1 August 1884 and the southern section on 1 May 1885. This view of a non-push and pull-fitted pannier tank hauling an auto trailer at Thorverton station on the southern side of Tiverton was taken on 2 March 1963. Most workings on this line were in the hands of auto-fitted 1400 Class 0-4-2Ts pushing or pulling two-coach trains, but when 5700 Class pannier tanks were sometimes substituted they had to run round the stock at the end of the line. Thorverton, with its passing loop, was one of the busiest passenger stations despite being located on the outskirts of the village and there was significant freight traffic generated by the nearby water mill, which had its own siding. Passenger services on the lightly used Exe Valley line were withdrawn on 7 October 1963 but freight services continued at Thorverton until 4 May 1964. The station building, obscured in this view by the signal box, is now a private residence in Silver Street appropriately named Beeching's Way.

On the same day he covered the Exe Valley line, Blake also photographed the 'Tivvy Bumper' push and pull at Halberton Halt, the only intermediate stop on the 4¾ mile line from Tiverton to Tiverton Junction in Devon on which there were still fourteen trains in each direction on weekdays. Opened by the B&ER in 1848, this short branch was originally broad gauge but was converted to standard gauge by the GWR in 1884. Despite a frequent service, the line closed to passengers on 5 October 1964 and to all traffic in June 1967. The line was constructed with double track in mind but was always single, conveniently giving space for Halberton Halt, which opened on 5 December 1927, to be sited beneath a wide overbridge. Locomotive No.1466 was built in 1936, withdrawn on 28 December 1963 and purchased by the 14XX Preservation Society (later becoming the Great Western Society) for £750. The price included movement in steam from its final shed at Taunton to the Society's base at Totnes Quay three months later. Previously always a West Country-based engine, No.1466 steamed out of Devon in December 1967 to its latest home at Didcot.

All three stations served by the 'Tivvy Bumper' are now closed. This includes Tiverton Junction where No.1466 is taking water before making the twelve minute journey back to Tiverton. The station was opened as Tiverton Road in 1844 and renamed Tiverton Junction when the Tiverton branch opened four years later. The station was also the terminus of the Culm Valley Light Railway to Hemyock, which closed to passengers in September 1963. Two miles north of Tiverton Junction, the GWR had opened a station at Sampford Peverell in 1932, which closed in 1964. A replacement station for Tiverton Junction was constructed on the site of Sampford Peverell station, close to the M5 motorway. The new station, called Tiverton Parkway, opened in 1986, whereupon Tiverton Junction was abandoned.

Until the Beeching Axe fell in the 1960s Langport in the Somerset Levels boasted two stations: Langport East on the Paddington-Penzance mainline via the Castle Cary 'cut-off' and the one shown here, Langport West on the branch to Yeovil, which opened in 1853. There is a campaign to reinstate Langport East station. The line through Langport West closed to passengers from 15 June 1964 and to goods a month later. At the time, there was strong local opposition to the withdrawal of the twenty-six mile Taunton to Yeovil Pen Mill service. During its latter days the six weekday trains plus an extra on Saturdays were worked by a variety of motive power, for example: small WR prairie tanks (in particular No.4593, which hauled the last passenger train), large WR prairie tanks (5101 Class), SR Class N moguls and Riddles Standard Class 3 tanks. The last of the latter class, Taunton-based No.82044, which had a short service life of just ten years before being scrapped, is seen on 7 December 1963 beside a droopy and vertically challenged signal at Langport West.

Yeovil originally boasted three railway stations but now has just two. The first station, Yeovil Pen Mill, was opened by the B&ER in 1856 and is served at the moment by trains running between Bristol Temple Meads and Weymouth via Castle Cary. In 1860 the LSWR opened Yeovil Junction between Salisbury and Exeter on its West of England mainline and in the following year a joint LSWR/GWR station called Yeovil Town opened. This was the most central and so best located of the stations, and ironically is the one that has closed, with passenger services withdrawn from 3 October 1966 and freight services twelve months later. Until dieselisation the three stations were linked by auto train services that, before the WR took over from the SR in 1963, had been worked by ex-LSWR M7 tanks. From March 1963, the WR introduced its style of auto trains worked usually by large wheeled 5400 Class or small wheeled 6400 Class pannier tanks and this view depicts No.6430 on 30 August 1964 about to leave Yeovil Pen Mill for Yeovil Town on the four-minute, half-mile journey. These locos were housed at Yeovil Town mpd, which closed to steam in June 1965.

This view of No.6430 was taken on the same day just outside Yeovil Town station. Behind the tree on the right was the 1¾ mile spur to Yeovil Junction that was also worked by auto trains. The Pen Mill service was withdrawn on 29 November 1965 and that to Yeovil Junction, as stated previously, on 3 October 1966. Redundant diesel railbuses from the Cirencester and Tetbury branches displaced the steam push and pulls and No.6430, together with its Yeovil-based sister No.6435, was withdrawn in October 1964. The Dart Valley Railway purchased No.6435 and also bought No.6430 from Cashmores, the scrap merchants, for spares. This engine, built at Swindon Works in 1937, is now on the Llangollen Railway and returned to steam in 2003. Yeovil still enjoys occasional visits by steam-hauled railtours because there is an operational turntable at Yeovil Junction and a preservation society (the Yeovil Railway Centre) is based there.

The cross-country Somerset & Dorset (S&D) line linking Bath to Bournemouth was formed in 1862 from an amalgamation of two separate companies that had built a railway from Burnham-on-Sea via Highbridge and Evercreech to Wimborne, the new company being called the Somerset & Dorset Railway. Using LSWR tracks, trains could reach Hamworthy, thereby linking the Bristol Channel to the English Channel. However, little traffic was generated, so the S&D built a northern extension from Evercreech to Bath, thus joining up with the Midland Railway (MR). Unfortunately the cost of the extension bankrupted the S&D, which leased the line to a joint committee of the MR and LSWR. MR provided the motive power and the LSWR was responsible for infrastructure and rolling stock, thus creating the Somerset & Dorset Joint Railway. At Highbridge, the S&D joined up with the GWR's Bristol-Taunton line and located its locomotive, carriage and wagon works there, as well as an engine shed. The works closed in 1930 but the mpd remained open until the S&D closed in March 1966. Blake visited the shed on 26 February 1966 when the service to Evercreech Junction had been cut to two trains per day. On shed were Ivatt Class 2 2-6-2Ts, Nos.41206 (an ex-LMS loco built in 1946) and BR-built 41307.

Scores of photographers recorded the slow death of the S&D. Freight withered away and then, because of regional boundary changes, the S&D section north of Templecombe transferred to the WR in 1958. Western locomotives were drafted in but, more importantly, the WR seemed intent on running down the line. Through trains to the south coast from the North and the Midlands were diverted away in September 1962 leaving only local services, so the S&D was listed for closure in the Beeching Report. After a brief reprieve due to problems over replacement buses, the much reduced services between Bath and Bournemouth and on the branch from Evercreech Junction to Highbridge (already cut back from Burnham-on-Sea in 1951 for normal services) were withdrawn from 7 March 1966. Blake took this view a couple of years earlier on 16 May 1964. Collett 0-6-0, No.2218 prepares to leave West Pennard on its way from Highbridge to Evercreech Junction, this original mainline section effectively having been downgraded to a branch following the opening of the extension to Bath in 1874.

Connecting with the GWR at Radstock, the S&D had a small engine shed there. It also had its own locomotive fleet that included seven Fowler 3F 0-6-0Ts (later nicknamed Jinties). These banked freight trains up to Masbury summit over the Mendip Hills and shunted in local collieries. No.47276, a Vulcan Foundry-built engine dating from 1924 and pictured here at Radstock on 30 December 1964, was not, however, a former S&D loco. During the 1950s it was employed as a Lickey Incline banker and transferred from Bromsgrove to Radstock in April 1964. It was withdrawn in March 1966 upon closure of the S&D.

During a visit to the S&D on 8 September 1962, Blake spotted this delightful oil lamp at Masbury, mounted on a piece of old rail.

This picture looking north at Evercreech Junction depicts ex-LMS 4F No.44422 (another Barry escapee that has recently moved to the West Somerset Railway) on a Bath to Templecombe service on 16 May 1964. Notice the S&D's idiosyncratic head lamp code that made no distinction between express and local passenger trains and also the tablet catcher for single line working attached to the tender. Although the S&D owned five Fowler 4F 0-6-0 tender engines, this was not one of them. Two former S&D locomotives do however survive, thanks to ending up in Dai Woodham's scrapyard at Barry, and these are 53808 and 53809 belonging to the unique 7F 2-8-0 Class.

This forbidding sign located at Evercreech Junction was photographed on 7 August 1965.

SOMERSET **AND** DORSET JOINT LINE.
TRESPASSING ON THE RAILWAY.

NOTICE IS HEREBY GIVEN THAT UNDER THE PROVISIONS OF THE
37TH SECTION OF THE SOUTH WESTERN RAILWAY ACT, 1902, ANY
PERSON WHO SHALL TRESPASS UPON ANY OF THE LINES OF
RAILWAY BELONGING OR LEASED TO OR WORKED BY THE
SOUTH WESTERN RAILWAY COMPANY IN CONJUNCTION WITH
THE MIDLAND RAILWAY COMPANY, SHALL ON CONVICTION
BE LIABLE TO A PENALTY NOT EXCEEDING 40/- & PUBLIC
WARNING IS HEREBY GIVEN TO PERSONS NOT TO TRESPASS
UPON THE RAILWAY.

DATED THIS 5TH DAY OF AUGUST 1903

GODFREY KNIGHT, } JOINT SECRETARIES.
WILLIAM CLOWER, }

It's refreshment time for engines in this view dating from 7 August 1965 at Evercreech Junction looking south. An Ivatt 2-6-2T is taking water close to where No.44422, depicted on the previous page, was standing while another, 41249, has three railwaymen attending to its every need. Unfortunately, despite all this activity there is little sign of passengers. Built at Crewe and entering service in November 1949, 41249 was transferred to Templecombe mpd in June 1965 where it was based when seen here attached to a WR Hawksworth coach and an SR Maunsell utility van. It was withdrawn and broken up following closure of the S&D in March 1966.

Another relic of the former Joint Railway at Blandford Forum was photographed on 5 March 1966.

In the south-east corner of Dorset lies the Isle of Purbeck, albeit not a true island but a peninsula surrounded almost entirely by water (River Frome, Poole Harbour, Studland Bay and the English Channel) apart from its short western inland boundary. Purbeck was served by a line from Wareham to the holiday resort of Swanage (now largely reopened as a heritage railway) and this picture illustrates an elderly Drummond Class M7 locomotive, No.30111, on the branch train at Wareham. This 0-4-4T clocked nearly sixty years of service, having been constructed at the LSWR's locomotive works at Nine Elms in March 1903 (six years before locomotive building was transferred to Eastleigh) and withdrawn in January 1964. During a visit on 9 September 1962, Blake recorded the engine taking on water, which appears to be going into the wrong place!

Also on 9 September 1962, 30111 is seen against the backdrop of the Purbeck Hills near Corfe Castle as it propels its train from Swanage back to Wareham. This highly successful class consisted of 105 locomotives built between 1897 and 1911. They were designed initially for hauling commuter trains on the Waterloo lines and except for one that was used for boiler experiments and another that fell down the Waterloo & City ('the Drain') lift shaft, the class remained intact until the first withdrawals occurred in 1957, a process that lasted until 1964.

Blake's Christmas/New Year visit to family in Northern Ireland (see page 160) in 1964-65 was cut short due to the impending dieselisation of the Swanage branch coinciding with a favourable weather forecast, despite the low temperature. This allowed him to visit on 28 December 1965 when he recorded Standard Class 4 2-6-4T, No.80146 on a Swanage bound train leaving Corfe Castle, the only intermediate station on the branch in BR days. The village takes its name from the Castle, which was originally built by William the Conqueror in the eleventh century and was largely demolished in 1646 by the Parliamentarians (Roundheads) during the English Civil War when it was a Royalist (Cavalier) stronghold. Brighton-built 80146 had the typically short service life of a BR Standard, clocking just under eleven years, having entered service in October 1956 and being withdrawn on 9 July 1967, the last day of steam operation on the SR.

The Swanage branch enjoyed reasonable service in steam days. Most departures were from Wareham but, in summer, some carriages destined for Swanage were detached from main line trains. On 20 June 1965, one such working is seen leaving Corfe Castle for Swanage behind Standard Class 4 2-6-0, No.76065 from Eastleigh mpd where the loco spent its entire short working life of barely nine years. Since the heritage Swanage Railway was connected in 2002 to the National Rail network at Motala, between Norden and Furzebrook, occasional through specials have come onto the branch. A trial diesel service into Wareham is scheduled to begin in Summer 2016. This follows the granting of a ninety-nine year lease to the Swanage Railway in September 2014 covering the existing 6½ miles from Swanage to Norden, replacing a shorter lease, plus the extra three miles up to the main line at Worgret Junction.

Yet another locomotive type used on the Swanage branch in BR days was the LMS Ivatt-designed Class 2 2-6-2Ts, represented here by No.41224 on 20 June 1965 near Harman's Cross. As mentioned previously, there was only one intermediate station, Corfe Castle, from the time when the branch opened in 1885 until it closed on 3 January 1972, but the heritage railway has since created extra stations at Norden, Herston and Harman's Cross. The branch escaped the Beeching Axe but was subsequently earmarked for closure in September 1968 despite being well used, especially in summer. The die was cast but, due to problems over replacement bus services, the line received a stay of execution until 3 January 1972 and the northern section from Motala, near Furzebrook, to Worgret Junction even remained open until 2005 for clay and oil traffic.

During an earlier visit on 20 June 1965, this scene was taken at the Swanage terminus. There was considerable local opposition to the loss of the line and a preservation society was quickly formed but faced many obstacles. In addition to the removal of three bridges, work had started on clearing the railway site at Swanage to make way for a shopping centre and demolition of the station building had begun (but luckily not completed). Furthermore, a bypass was scheduled to be built on railway land at Corfe Castle. Fortunately, as support for the fledgling society increased, both development plans were cancelled and a start was made on relaying track. The first passenger train ran over a few hundred yards of track in August 1979 but in 1982 Herston was reached followed by Corfe Castle in 1995. On its website the Swanage Railway reminds us it took seven weeks to lift 6½ miles of track and almost thirty years to relay it!

Still in Dorset (just) was Ashley Heath Halt on the section of the former Southampton & Dorchester Railway from Brockenhurst to Broadstone via Ringwood and Wimborne that opened in 1847. Promoted by a Wimborne solicitor, Charles Castleman, this circuitous twenty-five mile line nicknamed Castleman's Corkscrew became a secondary route when the coastal line through Bournemouth, a town of growing importance, was completed in 1888. Ashley Heath Halt was situated between Ringwood and West Moors stations and opened on 1 April 1927 to serve new residential areas. Although the line was used by summer excursions avoiding Bournemouth, it closed to passengers on 4 May 1964 when the eight or so weekday trains between Bournemouth West and Brockenhurst were withdrawn because of the Beeching Axe; however, freight trains over part of the line continued until the 1970s. One platform and station nameboard at Ashley Heath Halt survive as a feature on the Castleman Trailway, which uses the old trackbed. Here, on 31 July 1963, the push and pull train is being propelled by Class M7 0-4-4T, No.30048, a Bournemouth-based engine that had transferred from Exmouth Junction some three months earlier. It was withdrawn in January 1964 after fifty-eight years of service.

Crossing now to the Isle of Wight, a smart-looking Adams O2 0-4-4T approaches Ryde Esplanade station from Ryde Pier Head on 15 September 1963, with the sea almost up to the high water mark. No.18 *Ningwood* appears to have been guilty of spattering liquid over bystanders because its Westinghouse brake pump is covered by a protective shield! Until 1966, the Island was a steam paradise with veteran locos and elderly coaches recreating a lost world, but Dr Beeching had his axe poised over the remaining lines. During 1966, the service to Newport and Cowes closed in February followed by Shanklin to Ventnor in April and freight on both sections in May. Fortunately, the heavily used 8½ miles from Ryde Pier Head to Shanklin was reprieved. When steam haulage over this section finished on 31 December 1966 the line closed for the completion of third rail installation. It reopened using elderly ex-London Transport electric tube stock on 20 March 1967.

Ventnor at Ventnor! Class O2 0-4-4T, No.16 *Ventnor* takes on water at the terminus of the former Isle of Wight Railway line from Ryde. Carved out of an old quarry, the station site occupied a confined space immediately south of the 1,312yd tunnel through St Boniface Down (in the background). In 1923 the three Isle of Wight railway companies were absorbed into the SR, which began modernising and standardising the Island's locomotive fleet and rolling stock. The selected passenger locomotive type was the O2 Class, many of which were redundant following replacement on the mainland by more powerful tank engines such as the M7s. Between 1889 and 1895, sixty Class O2s were built by the LSWR at Nine Elms, of which twenty-three ended up on the Island including No.16 (ex-LSWR No.217), which was built in 1892 and eventually clocked seventy-four years of service.

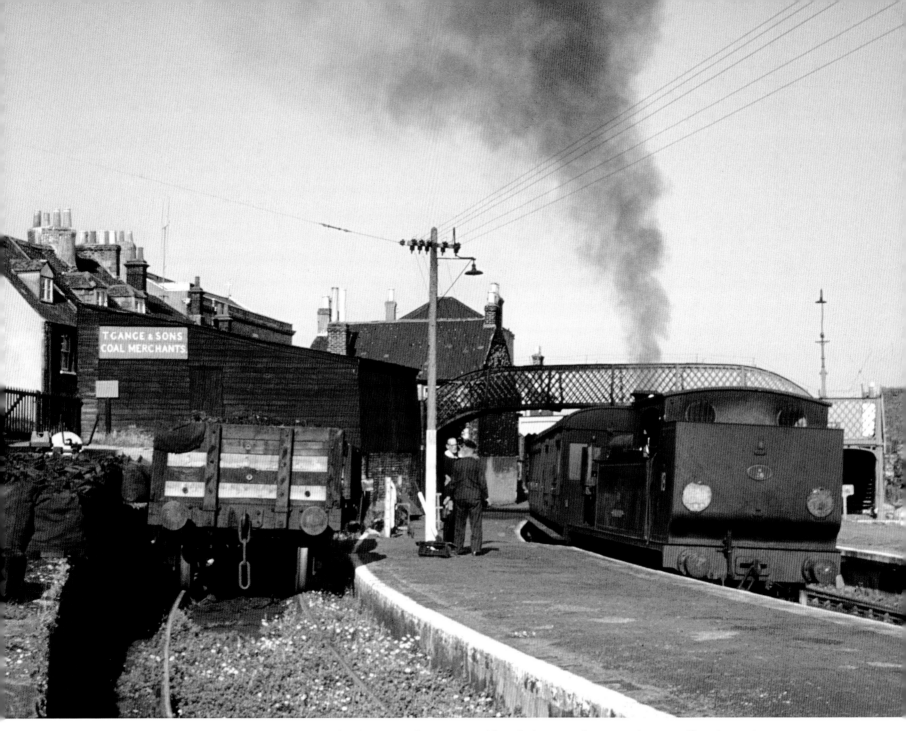

As previously stated, Cowes lost its passenger and freight service during 1966, although the 5½ mile section from Smallbrook Junction to Wootton has since been reopened by the heritage Isle of Wight Steam Railway. There is the possibility of an extension to the outskirts of Newport and/or to Ryde St John's Road. The Society owns the only surviving Class O2 locomotive (No.24 *Calbourne*). This photograph of No.18 *Ningwood* taken on 15 September 1963 captures all the charm of a lost age with the coal yard, and coal sacks serving as a reminder of the railway's role in delivering household fuel. The splendid footbridge is still in use, following its removal to Medstead & Four Marks station on the Mid-Hants Railway (Watercress Line). Isle of Wight locos escaped having BR smokebox number plates; they had bunker ones instead!

The Havant-Hayling Island branch in Hampshire was a favourite with enthusiasts. Opened to passengers by the London Brighton & South Coast Railway (LBSCR) on 16 July 1867, it was the final haunt of the ancient Stroudley 'Terriers' on BR metals when the last scheduled passenger train ran on 2 November 1963 (although ironically the heritage Bluebell Railway had by then been operating one in passenger service for more than three years). The 4½ mile branch, which carried exceptionally heavy loads during the summer (some trains being double-headed), made a small annual profit but was listed for closure by Beeching due to the deteriorating condition of the weak wooden bridge over Langstone harbour and the apparently unjustifiable cost of replacing it. This last day shot at Havant depicts No.32650, which was built in 1876 as No.50 *Whitechapel*. Between 1930 and 1936 it had worked on the Isle of Wight as W9 *Fishbourne*, after which it became the Lancing Carriage Works shunter numbered 515S. It was then used for oil burning experiments in 1946 before returning to normal duties. It is now owned by the London Borough of Sutton and was to be placed in their new civic centre but has remained on rails and is on loan to the Spa Valley Railway. Ironically, the last Terrier scrapped by BR, in September 1963, was the original *Sutton*, No.32661. The vehicle on the left of the picture is the unique fibreglass carriage, S1000S, now preserved on the East Somerset Railway and needing minimal maintenance.

There were two intermediate stations on the Hayling Island branch: Langston (called Langstone until 1873) and North Hayling. On 26 May 1963, Blake took this view of Terrier No.32646 leaving Langston on a southbound train. Between 1872 and 1880, 50 Stroudley Class A 0-6-0Ts were built for London suburban services but were soon replaced by larger locomotives and many were sold or scrapped. The first withdrawn by the LBSCR was No.72 *Fenchurch*, which was the oldest, having entered service on 9 September 1872. It was sold in 1898, reacquired by the SR in 1926, worked the farewell Hayling Island special on 3 November 1963 as No.32636, together with 32670 (see next page), and is now on the Bluebell Railway. No.32646 also had an interesting life that included being sold to the LSWR in 1903, working on the Isle of Wight from 1913-1949 as No.W8 *Freshwater* and standing on a plinth outside the Hayling Billy public house from 1966 to 1979 until donated by Whitbreads for use on the Isle of Wight Steam Railway.

No.32670 was almost ninety-one years old when it was recorded at Hayling Island station on 26 May 1963. This remarkable engine was the first of the class built but its entry into service was delayed because its cylinders were removed and fitted to No.71, which was experiencing problems. Entering service as No.70 *Poplar* on 4 December 1872, it was sold to the Rother Valley Railway (later the Kent & East Sussex Railway (K&ESR)) in May 1901, becoming No.3 *Bodiam*, which is also its latest identity following purchase from BR by the heritage K&ESR. The Class A tanks were reclassified A1 from 1905 and the survivors were rebuilt with improved boilers and longer smokeboxes from 1911 and designated Class A1X (the first to be treated, formerly No.78 *Knowle*, is also preserved on the K&ESR). Ten Terriers survive out of the fifty built, three of which have the appearance of A1s, with original style short smokeboxes and wingplates. These are the Bluebell Railway's No.72 *Fenchurch*, the National Railway Museum's No.82 *Boxhill* and the Canada National Railway Museum's No.54 *Waddon*.

Venturing inland to Sussex for views of the 'Cuckoo Line' linking Eridge to Polegate, diesel electric multiple unit (DEMU) No.1310 is seen at Hellingly, just north of Hailsham, on 5 April 1964. This station was opened on 1 September 1880 by the LBSCR and became a junction when the Hellingly Hospital Railway was constructed in 1899. The LBSCR station had only one platform and a wooden transfer platform was constructed facing the station building on the site of the grassy bank to the right of the train. The hospital branch was electrified in 1902 using a single overhead wire and closed to passengers in 1931, whereupon the platform was removed, but freight operations continued on the branch until 1959. Hellingly station closed from 14 June 1965 when the section of the 'Cuckoo Line' from Eridge to Hailsham was axed following the Beeching Report. This was despite carrying reasonable traffic on the relatively frequent service between Eastbourne and Tunbridge Wells West. The Hailsham to Polegate section survived until September 1968. Hellingly station house is now a private residence and unusually still retains the platform and canopies; the Cuckoo Trail footpath/cycleway passes alongside.

The second station north of Hellingly on the 'Cuckoo Line' was Heathfield, which had a large goods depot that remained open until 5 August 1968. This view of a pick-up freight leaving Heathfield and heading south towards Hailsham was taken on 10 June 1965, just days before the end of the passenger service. In charge is Standard Class 4 2-6-4T, No.80141, which was built at Brighton Works and entered service in July 1956. It saw barely 9½ years of service, being withdrawn in January 1966 and representing another scandalous waste of money.

On 10 June 1965, Blake also photographed Standard Tank No.80019 from Redhill mpd at Heathfield on a Tunbridge Wells West-Eastbourne service, the journey time being about one hour and twenty minutes. At this time, trains on the line were steam-hauled on Mondays to Fridays, and DEMUs worked the weekend services. The station house on Station Approach (the large gabled building above the platform building) is a private residence and the booking office (the attached single storey building) is now a shop. The tunnel has been incorporated into the Cuckoo Trail. The railway was nicknamed the 'Cuckoo Line' by virtue of the Heffle Fair held at Heathfield every April, Heffle being an old local name for Heathfield. Following a custom that originated in 1315, a cuckoo is supposed to be released from a basket at the Fair to mark the arrival of spring.

Still on the 'Cuckoo Line', DEMU No.1310 waits at Mayfield on 5 April 1964. Located two stops south of Eridge, this was typical of so many stations that were too far from centres of habitation and consequently little used. The trackbed and platforms here have made way for the Mayfield bypass but the main station building survives as a private residence perched above the road. No.1310 was built at Eastleigh in 1962 and belonged to a fleet of nineteen such three-car sets for operation on the Oxted line. These units, nicknamed 'Thumpers', were later designated as BR Class 207 with some remaining in service until 2004. Three units have been preserved including 1317, which is based on the heritage Spa Valley Railway and operates into Eridge, as it would have done during its BR life.

Moving to south-east Kent, both the Ashford-Hastings line and the 13½ mile branch from Appledore to New Romney were listed for closure in the Beeching Report. The former was reprieved but the latter, known locally as 'The Ponderosa' line, closed to passenger traffic on 6 March 1967, although access to the power station at Dungeness was retained. Between Appledore and Lydd Town, the fourteen level crossings were manned mostly by female employees who occupied primitive cottages, many of which had no running water, gas or electricity. Blake visited this windswept area on 4 February 1967, by which time the service was usually worked by a BR Eastleigh-built DEMU dating from 1958, one of which, No.1119, is seen at Brookland halt. This was another station located some distance from habitation, with most locals opting to use more convenient bus services. Once there had been a passing loop and signal box but latterly, only the up platform with its small hut was used; however, the buildings on the down platform were in situ. Tickets were obtained from a porter who resided in another hut near the level crossing from where he operated the crossing gates.

The Appledore-Dungeness line opened in 1883 with the branch from Lydd to New Romney following in 1884. For many years, passengers on some trains heading to and from New Romney had to alight at Lydd while their train made a return trip to Dungeness. This situation continued until 1937, the year in which the Lydd-New Romney branch was realigned by the Southern Railway to run nearer to the coast. Two new stations then opened to serve a holiday camp and a growing number of bungalows. Anticipating heavy summer traffic, Lydd-on-Sea originally had an island platform but the loop was seldom used. It ended its days as a little-used halt on an exposed stretch of shingle. Blake took this view of No.1119 on 4 February 1967.

The other new station opened in 1937 was Greatstone-on-Sea, which was close to a holiday camp but with the growth in coach travel, private car ownership and overseas holidays during the 1950s and 1960s it too became an unstaffed halt. Even the introduction of an improved service in 1962 failed to save this branch. Latterly, there was a train about every two hours on weekdays with extras at peak hours and on summer Saturdays, plus three return workings on summer Sundays. Interestingly, passengers boarding here and at Lydd-on-Sea had to purchase their tickets at Lydd Town.

The station at New Romney and Littlestone-on-Sea was mostly used by visitors including those heading for the nearby narrow gauge Romney, Hythe & Dymchurch Railway. Nearly all departures ran through to Ashford, a distance of twenty-two miles. Passenger services ended on 6 March 1967. Before this all pick-up goods had also stopped. Among other things these had transported flint shingle, materials to and from a military establishment at Lydd, agricultural produce, sheep and newborn chicks.

WITHDRAWAL OF RAILWAY PASSENGER SERVICES
Appledore to New Romney & Littlestone-on-Sea

Railway passenger services between Ashford (Kent) and New Romney & Littlestone-on-Sea and all railway passenger services between Appledore and New Romney & Littlestone-on-Sea will be withdrawn, and the following stations closed:

BROOKLAND HALT	GREATSTONE-ON-SEA HALT
LYDD TOWN	NEW ROMNEY & LITTLESTONE-ON-SEA
LYDD-ON-SEA HALT	

on and from Monday, 9 January 1967, subject to the granting of the necessary road service licences by the Traffic Commissioners for the alternative bus services

Returning to Sussex, Class H 0-4-4T, No.31544 hauls a push and pull train on the Three Bridges-East Grinstead (High Level) branch on 7 October 1962. It has just left the isolated and little-used station of Rowfant, one of two intermediate stations. The original building, dating back to the opening on 9 July 1855, can be seen behind the carriages. The railway passed through the estate of Curtis Miranda Lampson, an Anglo-American fur merchant, who made access conditional on having what was, in effect, his own personal station at Rowfant. In 1866 the line was extended from East Grinstead to Groombridge and Tunbridge Wells (the latter section now forming part of the heritage Spa Valley Railway). This was another Beeching casualty that, despite having an hourly service worked by DEMUs, eventually closed in the face of strenuous local opposition on 2 January 1967. Locomotive No.31544 was one of five H Class tank engines that served as air raid shelters for shed staff during the Second World War, although there is speculation over whether this function was achieved by plating over the cab sides or by stationing them over inspection pits and placing sandbags around the frames and wheels.

Blake photographed a problem that appeared to have arisen at Rowfant on 7 October 1962. What happened becomes evident overleaf but suffice to say it resulted in Class K 2-6-0, No.32347, which was allocated to Three Bridges, being dispatched to the goods yard. This much mourned class of seventeen Billinton-designed mixed traffic locomotives built between 1913 and 1921 for the LBSCR remained intact until officialdom, concerned that the Southern Region's withdrawal programme was falling behind, immediately withdrew the entire class irrespective of their condition or usage. Following this extraordinary decision in November and December 1962, all the engines were broken up. The original intention was for twenty to be constructed but the final three were not produced because, following the Grouping in 1923, the newly formed Southern Railway preferred the S15 and N classes for mixed traffic work; arguably the K Class turned out to be just as successful.

No.32347 has been sent to Rowfant to rescue No.31308, which appears to have suffered a defect while operating a passenger service. Industrial premises now occupy this site and the signal box and crossing gates have gone, but the stationmaster's house (visible behind the signalbox) is now a private residence and the attractive station building on the right remains intact. The platform side is not accessible, being within a commercial site, but it is possible to walk past the rear of this structure along the Worth Way footpath/cycleway that occupies much of the trackbed between Three Bridges and East Grinstead. Dr Beeching lived at East Grinstead but that did not stop him from axing his local branch, although it may have helped save the East Grinstead-Oxted service on which the good doctor happened to be a first-class season ticket holder!

Having watched the railwaymen examining the inner workings of the ailing 0-4-4, these well-dressed children carry out their own inspection and seem to have identified the problem! The H Class consisted of sixty-six engines designed by Wainwright for the South Eastern & Chatham Railway (SECR) for use on London suburban services and were built between 1904 and 1909 (apart from two found in kit form in 1915 and assembled then). No.31308 was built at Ashford Works and entered service in June 1906. Its indisposition on 7 October 1962 may have been terminal because the locomotive was withdrawn two months later; some class members lasted up to January 1964, such as the sole survivor, 31263, which is on the Bluebell Railway.

On the subject of survivors, here is Class M7 0-4-4T, No.30053. Built at the LSWR's Nine Elms Works in 1905, this locomotive was not withdrawn until May 1964 and three years later was shipped to the Steamtown museum in Vermont, USA. Repatriated in 1987, it now operates on the Swanage Railway, one of its old haunts. Another M7, No.30245, belongs to the National Railway Museum. On 24 February 1963, 30053 approaches Grange Road from Rowfant, these being the only two intermediate stations between Three Bridges and East Grinstead.

Although located in the village of Crawley Down, the station was called Grange Road (also the name of the adjacent street). The name was a sop by the LBSCR to the owner of the nearby mansion, *The Grange*, for his disappointment at receiving only about a quarter of the compensation he had demanded because of the original railway company refusing his request to build a tunnel under his estate. The station opened in 1860, five years after services started, and the station house, on the right of the picture, was built in 1876. There is no trace of the station site today, which is now occupied by a housing development with the address of Old Station Close and a parade of shops has been built across the gap alongside the existing shops and flats visible behind the engine. The gabled building across Station Road is The Royal Oak public house. This view looking east dates from 7 April 1963, by which time No.31544 looks considerably worse than it does on page 56. Unlike Rowfant, Grange Road was well used and patronage today would be considerably greater with the expansion of housing in Crawley Down in the 1970s.

It is not absolutely clear why this Maunsell Class U 2-6-0 is about to couple up tender first but this scene is rich in atmosphere, with parcels strewn across the platform and an elderly couple seated with their suitcases. The location is Guildford, looking north-east towards London/Reading on 20 June 1964. The locomotive, No.31790, is interesting because it was the prototype K Class 2-6-4 express passenger tank built by the SECR in 1917. A further twenty were constructed by the SR in 1925-26 and named after rivers in their territory, with the prototype becoming *River Avon*. The rationale for building express 2-6-4 tanks was the need for powerful engines with low axle loadings to operate on the weak and poorly maintained former SECR mainlines. Unfortunately, the engines were rough riders, and unstable at high speeds. A sequence of minor derailments culminated in the Sevenoaks disaster of 1927 when thirteen people were killed due to the derailment of No.800 *River Cray*. Consequently, all twenty-one were rebuilt in 1928 as mixed traffic tender engine 2-6-0s and classified U (and a single U1). One tank engine rebuild was lucky to end up at Woodhams scrapyard, this being No.31806 (formerly *River Torridge*), now on the Mid-Hants Railway.

Guildford was served by three rival pre-grouping railway companies: the LSWR from Woking and Effingham Junction to the South Coast, the LBSCR from Horsham and the SECR from Tonbridge and Redhill to Reading. A train working a service on the latter route is seen leaving Guildford for Reading hauled by Maunsell Class U 2-6-0, No.31633 from Guildford mpd. This locomotive was a new build, as opposed to a rebuilt River Class tank as referred to in the previous caption, and was constructed at Ashford in 1931. Despite its smart outward appearance, the locomotive was withdrawn in December 1963 and was not one of the four preserved members of the class to have the good fortune of ending up in Woodhams scrapyard at Barry.

This is Staines West, terminus of the WR's 6¼ mile branch from West Drayton & Yiewsley, photographed some eighteen months before the single track line closed to passengers on 27 March 1965. The goods shed on the right had been disused since general freight services ended in 1953, although the branch is still open today for bulk stone and aviation fuel trains as far as Colnbrook. On the left almost buried in the grass is the body of a GWR Toad brakevan. However, this is not so much a case of toad in the hole but toad over the hole, as it was apparently placed above the well that supplied the water tank! Beyond the Toad there was a small engine shed that closed in 1952 and was subsequently demolished, motive power being subsequently supplied from Southall shed. The station's name was Staines, as was the SR's separate station, so, following nationalisation, British Railways (BR) renamed the WR station Staines West and the SR station Staines Central. An oil storage depot opened on the site of the goods yard in October 1964 and a connection laid to the SR's Windsor line for tanker trains. This was because the M25 motorway was built over part of the trackbed between Staines West and Colnbrook. The oil depot closed in 1991 and houses have now been built on the site.

Looking out on what was once the front garden of a Georgian villa before its conversion into Staines West station (the back of the station had been the front of the house), a Pressed Steel single DMU stands at the platform after arriving from West Drayton. The buffer stops appear to have been fortified to protect the station building, from damage in the event of a train overrunning (as happened at Tattenham Corner in 1993, when the station building was wrecked). The canopy valance seen here is of typical Great Eastern Railway (GER) design, due to the contractor being accustomed to working for that railway company. The villa/station is now in its third incarnation, having been converted into smart offices.

When the Staines West branch opened in 1885, Colnbrook was the only intermediate station but several wayside halts were later added, the last in 1961. This busy scene at Poyle Halt for Stanwell Moor (dating from 1927) was taken in September 1963. From October 1958, diesel units had replaced 1400 Class-hauled auto trains and ex-GWR diesel railcars. There was a good service of about eighteen weekday trains taking on average just under twenty minutes. As part of a special heritage weekend, First Great Western ran shuttle trains between West Drayton and Colnbrook on 18 and 19 October 2014, giving passengers a unique opportunity to travel over the surviving freight-only section of the line.

This may look like an ordinary scene with a clockwork Jinty (see the key hole in the sidetank!) coupled to a brakevan, but it is probably the rarest picture in the book, due to its location. This Cricklewood-based Fowler 3F 0-6-0T has come from Brent Sidings on 25 September 1962 by way of South Acton, Acton Lane and the London Transport District Line to access the former Midland Railway (MR) coal yard next to Platform 4 of High Street, Kensington Underground Station. The MR had acquired an interest in the District Railway's Richmond extension, which allowed it to bring coal traffic into central London and had opened this depot in 1878. There was a steep incline from the low level Underground tracks to the street level yard, needing wagons to be propelled up by the locomotive. Latterly, the yard was used mainly for transporting building materials, with a scheduled train on Tuesdays and Thursdays arriving at 9.49am and departing at 3.23pm. The yard closed on 25 November 1963 and the Copthorne Tara Hotel now stands on the site.

Thompson Class L1 2-6-4T, No.67730, working a service on the ex-Great Eastern Railway (GER) North Woolwich-Palace Gates line, calls at Stratford Low Level on 5 May 1962. Services from Stratford to North Woolwich started in 1847 and the branch from Seven Sisters to Palace Gates opened in 1878. This latter branch closed to passengers on 7 January 1963 but services continued to North Woolwich until 9 December 2006, originating from Richmond. Stratford Low Level is now completely rebuilt and is unrecognisable from this view. Platforms 1 and 2 shown here are now platforms 16 and 17 and used by Docklands Light Railway trains. Palace Gates refers to Alexandra Palace ('Ally Pally') near Wood Green, to which the Great Northern Railway (GNR) had built a branch, and against which the GER wanted to compete. No.67730 belonged to a class of 100 built for the London & North Eastern Railway (LNER) between 1946 and 1950, all of which were withdrawn by the end of 1962.

Heading west, the country branch between Oxford-Fairford was a pre-Beeching closure latterly reduced to a few weekday trains, most of which ran with only a handful of passengers. By this time, the usual motive power on the twenty-two mile line (measured from Yarnton Junction) consisted of 5700 Class pannier tanks such as No.9654 seen here on 2 June 1962 or 2251 Class 0-6-0 tender engines. The latter class did not have to travel backwards because Fairford had a turntable where even the panniers were normally turned. Fairford was built to serve as a through station on a projected line to Cirencester where it was meant to join up with the Midland & South Western Junction Railway to Cheltenham. This was never realised, leaving the line to terminate among fields. The branch was originally opened in two stages by different companies: Oxford-Witney in 1861 by the Witney Railway Company and Witney-Fairford in 1873 by the East Gloucestershire Railway. This extension led to the opening of a new station at Witney with the original terminal station being closed for passenger traffic and turned over to freight use.

Passenger and freight services were withdrawn from Fairford on 18 June 1962. Blake took this view of the busy goods yard during his visit exactly a fortnight before. The passenger locomotive, No.9654, has been turned on the 55ft turntable and is taking on water while, in the foreground, fellow Pannier Tank No.4649, on a freight working, is attached to a Toad Brake Van, standing just clear of the timber engine shed. Witney, the principal station on the branch, remained open for freight until 2 November 1970, the thrice weekly trains to Hinksey Yard being diesel-hauled following the last steam working on 30 December 1965.

Pannier Tank No.9654 is now ready to leave Fairford for Oxford on the 1.50pm service. The original purpose of the branch was to connect the woollen town of Witney to the mainline railway network, the connection being made at Yarnton (remember the cast iron urinal on the up platform?). Yarnton was a station on the former Oxford, Worcester & Wolverhampton Railway and was also joined by a spur to the London & North Western's Oxford-Bletchley line. However, passengers travelling from Oxford to Worcester today will see no evidence that Yarnton station or junction existed. Indeed, every station on the Fairford branch has been obliterated except the utilitarian structure at Carterton that, with the addition of wooden cladding to the outer walls, has been converted into riding stables.

Many stations and halts were still lit by gas or oil in the 1960s but most succumbed to the Beeching Axe. The survivors were modernised, which inevitably included the installation of electric lighting. This seemingly Victorian scene, captured on 17 October 1964, exactly a fortnight before the halt closed, depicts a railwayman attending to the oil lamps at St Mary's Crossing Halt, near Chalford, on the Swindon to Gloucester/Cheltenham Spa line. Although the halt has vanished, the crossing is still there, its gates worked manually by the signalman in the adjacent signal box. The crossing gives access, via an unnamed road that turns off the A419 London Road, to St Mary's Mill, a former textile mill built about 1820 with a water wheel, which is occasionally open to the public. Several businesses are also on the mill site, so the crossing keeper is kept relatively occupied.

In latter days, the steam-worked auto trains operating between Gloucester and Chalford became a magnet for photographers. There were about a dozen workings on weekdays with four on Sundays (pm only). Journey time for the sixteen mile trip was just over forty minutes. The auto trains had been introduced in 1903 and heralded the introduction of railmotors (in effect a steam powered carriage – see the Great Western Society's restored No.93 based at Didcot). Known as 'The Golden Valley' line, this view taken between Brimscombe and Stroud illustrates the point. 1400 Class 0-4-2Ts hauling or propelling one or two trailers provided the bulk of the services but sometimes a non-auto-fitted pannier or prairie tank would be used, as depicted here on 17 October 1964 by Hawksworth Pannier Tank No.9471. Being unable to propel the auto trailers, the locomotive has run round at Chalford and is returning bunker-first to Gloucester. No.9471 spent its entire, but relatively short, service life at Gloucester Horton Road mpd, being allocated there when new in April 1952 and withdrawn from there a few days after Blake took this memorable view.

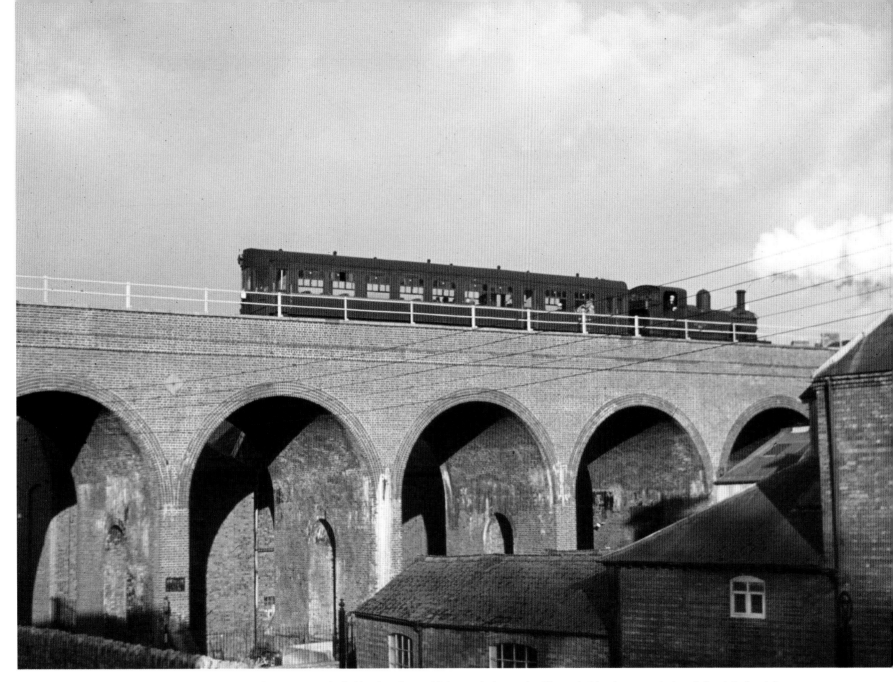

Stroud was the largest town between Gloucester and Chalford and, in addition to being a significant habitation, was industrialised. Indeed, it was one of the earliest cloth manufacturing areas in Britain, a trade originating in the fourteenth century. Before the opening of the railway, transportation was reliant on the Thames & Severn Canal that flowed through the town. The Viaduct, sometimes referred to as Capel Mill Viaduct (the mill was demolished when the brick viaduct was built in 1868), replaced a timber structure constructed when the line opened in the 1840s. In this view the 'Chalford Flyer' powered by a 1400 Class 0-4-2 tank has just propelled its Gloucester-bound train out of Stroud station. The viaduct, which spans the River Frome, the canal and the A46 Stroud bypass (the road is called Merrywalks), still carries trains but the buildings at ground level on the right have been replaced by a multi-storey car park fronted by vegetation, although the building visible through the arches still exists. The road passes through the railway arch previously used by the canal, which has only recently been diverted through another arch as part of a restoration project.

The driver and guard wait for Blake to take his picture at Ham Mill Halt and rejoin the auto train to Gloucester on 12 October 1963. Originally named Ham Mill Crossing Halt until 1957, it was one of seven installed between Gloucester and Chalford, all of which were closed when this well patronised local stopping service was withdrawn on 2 November 1964. In addition to the halts, there were stations at Stonehouse, Stroud, Brimscombe and Chalford, but only the first two are still open today. Whereas some of the halts had GWR pagoda shelters on the platforms, others such as Ham Mill had more rudimentary corrugated iron huts. The halt took its name from the nearby Ham Mill at Thrupp, which was founded in 1608 for cloth making. From 1900 to 1999, the Mill, in rebuilt form, was used for carpet weaving and there are proposals to renovate the Grade II listed buildings and construct fifty houses and fifty-two apartments on the site.

Contrasting with Gloucester to Chalford, auto trains on the 4¼ mile Berkeley Road to Sharpness service made just three trips in one direction and four in the other, resulting in virtually empty trains. In reality, this was a surviving limb of a one-time service linking the two sides of the Severn Estuary. This view dating from 12 October 1963 depicts a 1400 Class 0-4-2 tank beside the water tower at Sharpness station. Behind the steam, up on the hill, is the Severn Bridge and Railway Hotel, now a residential home, but no longer overlooking the ex-GWR/MR joint station that has vanished. Until 1967, the hotel also overlooked the latterly wrecked Severn Bridge, which was demolished in that year. This bridge was an important cross-river link between Berkeley Road, on the MR Gloucester-Bristol main line and Lydney Junction and the Forest of Dean. It was also used by diverted main line trains when the Severn tunnel was closed. All this ended on 25 October 1960 when two loaded petroleum vessels collided when trying to find the entrance to Sharpness Docks and dislodged one of the bridge piers. Two of the spans containing the railway lines crashed down, whereupon the tankers caught fire, setting the estuary alight, and five of the eight crew from the two boats died. The track to the Severn Bridge passed through the brick bridge beyond the station. 'Fourteeners' towed large ex-GWR locomotives to Coopers Metals at California sidings, Sharpness Docks, for scrapping, so the engine may have just returned from the docks after one such duty, or was simply shunting there, as its auto trailer is not in evidence.

On 12 October 1963, Blake also photographed the Sharpness push and pull at the branch platform at Berkeley Road. The train consisted of a 1400 Class 0-4-2T and one of the twelve auto trailers with driving vestibules converted in 1953 from Collett non-corridor compartment brake thirds. The need for these extra trailers arose from the introduction of auto trains in the Cardiff valleys, which also resulted in fifteen small prairie tanks (4575 Class) being fitted for push and pull working. Immediately following the Severn Bridge disaster, branch trains were cut back from Lydney Junction to Sharpness, which had been the original terminus when the branch opened to passengers in 1876 until the Severn Bridge was completed in 1879. The line was singled as early as 1931, resulting in derelict platforms at Sharpness (see previous picture) and also at Berkeley, the only intermediate station on the eastern side of the estuary. Passenger services were withdrawn on 2 November 1964 (the same day as the 'Chalford Flyer') under the Beeching Axe but the line remains open for the occasional freight working to Sharpness Docks. The fledgling Vale of Berkeley Railway plans to re-open the branch as a tourist attraction.

Berkeley Road, which opened in 1844 as Dursley and Berkeley Road, survived the withdrawal of passenger services on the Sharpness branch, but only for a few weeks. Although the Gloucester to Bristol line is very much still open, the intermediate stations such as Berkeley Road and Stonehouse (Bristol Road) (but not Stonehouse (Burdett Street) on the Chalford line) were closed following the withdrawal of local passenger services under the Beeching Axe on 4 January 1965; freight facilities at Berkeley Road lasted until 1 November 1966. This photograph, taken on 12 October 1964 looking towards Gloucester, shows Fowler 4F 0-6-0, No.44466 from Bristol (Barrow Road) mpd approaching on a stopping service. This engine entered service in 1928 and was withdrawn in May 1965. The National Railway Museum's preserved Fowler 4F, No.44027, is currently undergoing restoration at Sharpness for future use on the branch.

We are moving now to South Wales and to Treherbert, which today is the terminus of the twenty-three mile Rhondda line from Cardiff. Until 1962, trains also arrived here from Swansea and, up to 1968, from Bridgend, both services using the Rhondda Tunnel (1899) that was nearly two miles long. Bulk movement of coal was the main source of revenue but this traffic had been in decline since the end of the Second World War. Seen at the station on 9 May 1964 was No.4222, one of a group of powerful 2-8-0T engines designed by George Churchward to handle heavy goods, especially coal, principally in South Wales. These were the only 2-8-0T engines operated by BR. Keeping a watchful eye is the stationmaster, and on the opposite platform is a BRUTE (British Railways Universal Trolley Equipment) trolley. These carried pre-sorted merchandise and parcels that were loaded directly onto an assigned train.

Since 1863, the Neath-Pontypool Road line had been operated by the GWR and for many years carried heavy mineral traffic. On 21 September 1963, 0-6-0PT, No.4688 has arrived from Neath Riverside and is taking water at Hirwaun (previously Hirwain until 1928) before departing eastwards towards Aberdare and Pontypool Road. By this time, the passenger service consisted of a handful of lightly loaded journeys. Steam-hauled auto trains had once linked Hirwaun to Merthyr Tydfil. The Welsh Assembly is considering proposals to restore passenger services between Aberdare and Hirwaun.

The most impressive railway structure in South Wales was lofty Crumlin Viaduct completed in 1857. This engineering masterpiece spanning the steeply sided Ebbw Valley was a 'must' for photographers. Built by the Newport, Abergavenny & Hereford Railway as part of its Taff Vale Extension to Quaker's Yard, the heavily engineered section from Pontypool Road to Nelson & Llancaiach featured tunnels, massive earthworks, three valley crossings and several significant junctions. The Pontypool Road to Neath Riverside service had twenty-nine stopping places including several unadvertised colliery platforms. Journey time for the forty-two miles was a leisurely two hours or so. With the viaduct as a backdrop, a typical two-coach train hauled by a 5600 Class 0-6-2T waits to depart from Crumlin High Level on a 'down' train to Neath on 28 March 1964.

This view is from the west end of the viaduct on which the track had been singled by the GWR in the 1920s. This was due to the suspected fragility of the structure, particularly in high winds, given the increased weight of locomotives and their trains, as well as maintenance costs. Immediately below the tracks was a walkway, made famous by Sophia Loren and Gregory Peck in the dramatic penultimate sequence of the 1966 film *Arabesque*, and infamous when local children threw eggs on to passing buses below! Heading a long rake of coal empties on 28 March 1964 is 0-6-0PT, No.4639. During the First World War, millions of tons of coal en route to the naval base at Scapa Flow had crossed the viaduct.

During his visit on 28 March 1964, Blake also walked down to the valley to take a series of impressive views looking up at the viaduct. This one is of a Hawksworth pannier tank on an 'up' train to Pontypool Road. Designed and built of tubular steel and iron by T.W. Kennard, the 1,658ft long structure was in two sections. From the west side and crossing to a hillock on the valley side, 'little bridge' was 854ft long and rested on three giant spans, and 'big bridge' was 1,066ft long and crossed the valley itself on a further seven spans. Towering some 210ft above the valley bottom, this was the highest railway bridge in Britain and the third highest in the world. The Railway Hotel is still standing.

After the loss-making passenger service closed from 15 June 1964, the viaduct fell into disuse and despite preservation attempts was dismantled in 1967. During its life, stress levels were regularly tested by running two coupled locomotives onto the bridge while they made several stops. Here, a large Prairie Class 2-6-2T rumbles across the valley with an 'up' mixed goods on 28 March 1964. The Western Welsh Atlantean is en route for Newport and the delivery lorry advertises 'Gayday' drinks. The bus company began life as South Wales Commercial Motors and was renamed after the GWR transferred bus services to it in 1927 and became a shareholder.

The small steel town of Dowlais Cae Harris was reached by a steeply graded, double track 9½ mile branch from Nelson & Llancaiach. Opened in 1876, it gave rail access to a local iron works. To tackle grades of up to 1:40 some loaded ore trains had a loco at the front, one in the middle and one at the rear. The relatively infrequent passenger service was mostly used by schoolchildren and employees at the iron works, with trains running to and from either Nelson & Llancaiach, Hengoed (High Level) or Ystrad Mynach. Latterly there were about six weekday trains supplemented by extras on Saturday nights. The extras did at least carry lucrative payloads whereas weekday trains increasingly ran without fare-paying passengers. Traffic on the branch became the preserve of 5600 Class 0-6-2T engines, one of which is resting between duties on 21 September 1963. The closure from 15 June 1964 encountered virtually no local opposition.

The ninety-five mile Central Wales line from Swansea Victoria to Craven Arms was listed for closure in the Beeching Report at an estimated annual saving of £200,000. However, only the twelve mile southern section as far as Pontarddulais was actually closed, with the last train leaving Swansea Victoria on 13 September 1964, after which the Central Wales service was diverted to terminate at Llanelli. On 18 May 1964, Blake took this view of 0-6-0PT, No.3671 inside Swansea Victoria. On the left is a rake of London Midland & Scottish Railway (LMS) coaches, a reminder of the line's previous London & North Western Railway (LNWR)/LMS ownership. At one time trains or through coaches would leave here for the North, the Midlands and London Euston. A leisure complex now stands on the site.

On leaving Swansea Victoria the railway hugged the shore of Mumbles Bay and then, just before swinging north, it crossed the famous Swansea & Mumbles Railway, noted for its high capacity trams, which was abandoned in 1960. Among the intermediate stations to close on 13 September 1964 was Gowerton South where 7400 Class 0-6-0PT, No.7446 waits to depart for Pontarddulais and Llandilo on 18 May 1964. Note the 'Fire Devil' (coke brazier and chimney beside the water column). Since 1891, the Central Wales line had been operated by the LNWR, although the section from Pontarddulais and Llandilo was jointly worked with the GWR. A small park now stands on the site of Gowerton South, which acquired its appendage to distinguish it from the former GWR station at Gowerton that is still open.

Among the Beeching casualties in West Wales was the single track line connecting Llandilo to Carmarthen, which opened in 1865 and eventually became part of the LNWR. There was considerable goods traffic to and from Pembroke Dock and during the summer it was used by many holiday 'extras' from the North West and Midlands en route to the coastal resorts of Pembrokeshire. However, by the late 1950s, revenue was much reduced and the base service consisted of three to four weekday trains. Just days before it closed, Blake travelled the fifteen mile line on 6 September 1963 behind 7400 Class 0-6-0PT, No.7439, a regular performer on the branch. At deserted Nantgaredig the LNWR Lower Quadrant signal is attached to an LMS concrete post. Complete closure took place from 9 September 1963. Today, the station house survives although much rebuilt.

As mentioned on page 85, the Beeching Report envisaged complete closure of the Central Wales line. However, the bulk of the route escaped the axe with trains diverted to Llanelli following closure of the southern portion from Pontarddulais to Swansea Victoria in June 1964. To reduce operating loss, radical changes were introduced on the eighty-three miles between Pontarddulais and Craven Arms in September 1965. Journey times were reduced by half an hour on the handful of weekday passenger workings and improved connections were made at Llanelli and Shrewsbury. During a trip aboard a Swindon-built two-car cross-country DMU on 27 March 1968, Blake hopped on and off to photograph many of the intermediate stations including Cynghordy and those on the following three pages.

Cilmery, south-west of Builth Wells, was one of a number of stations reduced to the status of an unstaffed halt. As late as the early 1950s, twenty goods trains a day had passed through this station. Then in 1960 it was announced that freight movements were to be increased by providing extra paths at the expense of the lightly loaded passenger service. However, once it had been agreed that closure would lead to considerable local hardship, the freight traffic withered away.

The 31½ miles from Llandrindod Wells to Craven Arms was single track throughout with no passing loops, making it one of the longest block sections in the country. Here the DMU stands at Penybont Station. The powerful headlight fitted below the destination box gave extra illumination. As part of the cost-cutting exercise, there were no railway telephones or telegrams over much of the line, although the handful of surviving signal boxes at road crossings and passing loops were connected to the GPO telephone network.

Hopton Heath is a few miles south-west of Craven Arms. Back in the mid-1960s it was claimed that only a couple of stations north of Llandovery took more than £5 a day in passenger fares and this was not one of them! This line was saved in 1964, probably because it was an election year and the line ran through several marginal constituencies. These BR Swindon-built cross-country DMUs (latterly BR Class 120) were a successful design and some remained in service until 1989. The fleet consisted of 194 coaches, comprising three-car sets plus spares, constructed between 1958 and 1961.

Some loss-making services were axed before publication of the Beeching Report. These included the meandering cross-country mid-Wales line linking Three Cocks Junction on the Hereford to Brecon line with Moat Lane Junction on the Welshpool to Machynlleth line. Although serving few centres of population, a journey along this 48¼ mile scenic 'gem' offered excellent panoramic views but in winter the terrain was bleak and unrelenting. Opened mostly during 1864, the line eventually became part of the Cambrian Railway and later, when under GWR control, extra halts were opened between the wars. However, passenger traffic was always light and, with the growth in road traffic during the 1950s, the line was clearly a candidate for closure. Latterly only two trains worked the full length in each direction supplemented by a few short workings mostly to and from Builth Road (Low Level). In this view Blake has captured considerable activity at Three Cocks Junction on 15 October 1962 with, on the left, workings to and from Moat Lane Junction, and on the right an arrival from Hereford, waiting to depart for Brecon. Both these services closed on 29 December 1962.

One of the few towns of any significance on the Three Cocks Junction to Moat Lane Junction line was Rhayader, some ten miles north of Builth Wells. By 1962, people had largely deserted the infrequent services, some of which did not even connect at the junctions, so it is not surprising that only a single passenger appears to have alighted from this northbound train. Blake just had time to take his view before rejoining the front coach, which appears empty. Latterly most trains were hauled by Ivatt Class 2 2-6-0s. Note the goods yard on the left and the imposing water column on the platform. This was probably installed to replenish locos hauling heavy First World War coal trains on the long run from South Wales to the giant naval base at Scapa Flow in Orkney, north of the Scotland mainland. The last freight movements on the mid-Wales line survived between Llanidloes and Moat Lane Junction until 1967.

At just under eighteen miles, the Gaerwen Junction to Amlwch line cut across Anglesey in a north-easterly direction serving several towns and villages en route to the coast. Opened progressively between 1864 and 1867, the single track line initially handled mineral traffic as well as agricultural produce including fertiliser. On the passenger side, DMUs were introduced in the mid-1950s. These proved popular with the public and generated extra traffic; however, when these units were transferred to other duties during the summers of 1963 and 1964, steam-hauled stock reappeared for the duration of the summer timetable. On 22 August 1964, Blake made a special point of recording these reinstated steam workings, some of which started from Bangor. Here, Ivatt Class 2 2-6-2T, No.41226 is waiting to depart on the thirty-six minute run to the junction. Note the non-standard station nameboard with lettering formed from rope.

Latterly there were seven weekday departures for Gaerwen Junction where passengers could change for Holyhead, Bangor and Chester. In this second view of Amlwch station, another Ivatt 2-6-2T, No.41233 is seen on 22 August 1964 just months before the passenger service was withdrawn on 5 December. Although pick-up goods traffic also ended, the branch was used by trains serving a chemical plant at Amlwch until 1993 after which the line was mothballed. Amlwch station was demolished in the 1980s but Llanerchymedd station now serves as a heritage centre for the Anglesey Central Railway, which plans to reopen the line.

The fifty-three mile cross-country link between Ruabon and Barmouth Junction (Morfa Mawddach) opened in stages between 1862 and 1870. Although passenger loadings were never heavy, the line came into its own during the summer season with packed holiday trains making for the Welsh coastal resorts. However, a steep drop in patronage in the 1950s ensured the line was included in the Beeching Report. Closure took place on 18 January 1965, although flooding at Carrog during the night of 10/11 December 1964 meant it was operated in two sections during its final weeks. It was in this period that Blake braved the elements on 28 December 1964 to travel overnight from London to ride the first train of the day over the truncated eastern portion from Ruabon to Llangollen. This proved a challenge for the driver and fireman on Pannier Tank No.3789 as it took them 1¼ hours to tackle Acrefair bank before finally limping into Llangollen.

In the bitter cold, the driver of No 3789 walks up the platform to discuss the situation with other railway staff. The absence of any onboard heating explains the snow on the roof of the carriages. Any passengers heading further west would have been directed onto rail replacement buses. Happily two sections of the Ruabon-Barmouth Junction line are now once again carrying passengers: the narrow gauge Bala Lake Railway operating for 4½ miles between Bala (Penybont) and Llanuwchllyn and the ten mile standard gauge Llangollen Railway that runs between Llangollen and Corwen East. Llangollen station remains the same today as it did fifty years ago. The former goods yard and carriage sidings were located out of sight beyond the end of the platforms.

The Worcester-Bromyard-Leominster line was authorised in 1861 and took thirty-six years to complete; hardly an encouraging start! Traffic was always sparse on the Bromyard-Leominster section and this closed to passengers on 15 September 1952, but the Worcester Shrubhill-Bromyard section struggled on until 5 September 1964, with a very limited service comprising more trains in one direction than the other and a slightly better service on Thursdays and Saturdays. In this view, GWR diesel railcar No.W20 stands at Knightwick. This vehicle was withdrawn in October 1962 and bought by the Kent & East Sussex Railway, forming their first fare-paying public train on 3 February 1974. There were thirty-eight GWR diesel railcars and a further two survive: sister vehicle No.22 preserved by the Great Western Society at Didcot and streamlined No.4 at the Steam Museum, Swindon.

For the final two years of Worcester-Bromyard passenger workings following withdrawal of the GWR diesel railcars, DMUs were used except for certain peak hour trips that were worked by a pannier tank and three carriages. On 29 August 1964, a week before closure, Blake recorded one of these duties. Here 5700 Class 0-6-0PT, No.8793 from Worcester depot is heading the 5.45pm Worcester Shrub Hill-Bromyard train and is depositing passengers on the weed-strewn platform at Leigh Court at 6.06pm. This station, along with the other two on the Bromyard arm (Knightwick and Suckley), opened on 1 March 1878. Since closure the Leigh Court station site has been almost obliterated, save for the derelict remains of the station building. Journey time for the 14½ mile service was about forty minutes.

There were two stations between Worcester (Foregate Street) and Bransford Road Junction, where the Bromyard branch diverged from the line to Malvern and beyond. These were Rushwick Halt and Henwick, the latter being the location of this picture. The line is still open to passengers but Henwick station has vanished, except for the signal box visible at the back of the train. Indeed this signal box and its adjacent Victorian outside toilet received national media attention after details relating to the public announcement of 'signalling problems' at Henwick on 6 February 2013 were leaked. The driver of a Hereford-London service, kept waiting by an adverse signal, couldn't make radio contact with the signalman and left his cab to investigate. Cries for help led him to the brick toilet and a jammed lock. Reinforcements were called who released the signalman by forced entry with a crowbar. The train, by now more than an hour behind schedule, then continued its journey and other delayed trains resumed their services following this 'in-convenience'!

This derelict-looking station, Blowers Green, was still open to passengers on 28 July 1962, but it was, not surprisingly, its last day. Blowers Green Halt, on the Oxford, Worcester & Wolverhampton Railway, opened in 1862 and was upgraded in 1878 when it was renamed Dudley Southside and Netherton, before assuming its original name of Blowers Green in 1921. The station officially closed on 30 July 1962 when passenger services between Dudley and Stourbridge Junction were withdrawn. However, a passenger service (the 'Dudley Dodger') passed through it on the Bumble Hill line from Dudley to Old Hill for a further two years and freight trains used the route until 1993, after which the line has been cocooned for a possible reopening for freight services. There is no evidence remaining of the scene shown here, apart from overgrown tracks, although the booking hall building on New Road (behind the photographer) still exists, albeit bricked up. The mouth of Blowers Green Tunnel beneath Dudley (part of which can be seen in the background) is now blocked by steel gates.

Moving across country now to Stamford in Lincolnshire, this is a view of the 'Seaton Flyer' push and pull service standing in the bay platform on 7 June 1965, ready to return to Seaton in the county of Rutland. This former LNWR branch with an intermediate station at Morcott was located on the through line from Rugby via Market Harborough and joined the Midland Railway's Leicester-Manton-Peterborough line at Luffenham. Stamford's fine station, now a Grade II listed building with services to Birmingham, Peterborough and Stansted Airport, was built in 1848 following the opening of the first (eastern) section of the Syston and Peterborough Railway (subsequently the Midland Railway) in 1846. From 1950 to 1966 it was called Stamford Town to distinguish it from the former GNR Stamford East station that closed in 1957 and whose services to Essendine, after being diverted to Stamford Town, ended in 1959. In this view, the 'Seaton Flyer' consists of Standard Class 2 2-6-2, No.84008 and two ex-LMS suburban coaches converted to push and pull driver operation. The 9¾ mile Stamford Town-Seaton service, which was Britain's last steam-hauled push and pull, made its final run on 4 October 1965 and, following brief dieselisation, was withdrawn on 6 June 1966.

This smart GNR trespass notice, apart from having been bombed by a bird to form an exclamation mark, was located on the ECML at Helpston. Unlike many pre-grouping and pre-nationalisation signs, it has not had the original company name painted out by BR. Both pictures on this page were taken on 7 June 1965.

What now would be a valuable artefact lies discarded on the station platform at Helpston, Cambridgeshire, on the Midland Railway's Syston and Peterborough line. This station opened as Helpstone on 2 October 1846, later becoming Helpston for Market Deeping and plain Helpston in 1912. The MR line at this point runs parallel with the East Coast Main Line (ECML), the southern end of which (London to Shaftholme Junction, near Doncaster) was completed by the GNR in 1850. The MR agreed with the GNR to transport materials for its new line on condition that the latter company did not build a station at Helpston and steal its passengers. However, there is no longer any station at Helpston, following closure of the MR one on 6 June 1966. There were separate signal boxes controlling the two level crossings, which are no more than about two car lengths apart, but the operation merged in the 1970s and only the former GNR box, located between the two sets of tracks, remains. There are plans to replace the crossings with a road bridge.

When the line from London to Cambridge opened in 1845 objections from a wealthy landowner meant it bypassed Saffron Walden. This was rectified in 1865 when the important market town was connected to the mainline at Audley End by a 1¾ mile branch that was then extended northwards in the following year to connect with The Stour Valley line at Bartlow. Traffic on this former Great Eastern Railway (GER) 7¼ mile link was heavy but after the Second World War both goods and passenger levels declined. In 1958 staffing levels were reduced and German-built diesel railbuses introduced. This view at Audley End was one of several taken on 23 November 1963.

Ashdon Halt was typical of scores of unstaffed wayside stations dotted about the country, this one closing in 1964. The Halt opened in 1911 and featured GER 2nd class five-compartment carriage No.342 dating from 1883, which was converted into this passenger shelter in 1916 (and which remarkably is still in situ today, albeit derelict). Passengers boarding here and at Bartlow as well as at Saffron Walden on Sundays purchased their tickets from the guard. The fifty-six seat railbuses had been built in Germany to BR specifications by Waggon und Maschinebau that incorporated many standard parts used in similar vehicles built for the Deutsche Bundesbahn. The five railbuses were imported into Britain via the Zeebrugge-Harwich ferry. All had a relatively short life, the last being withdrawn in April 1967, although four have been preserved. This was one of three to have its German engine replaced by an AEC unit and to receive the yellow warning panel at the front.

Unlike so many other lines condemned by Beeching, this one enjoyed a good level of service and trains were well used in peak hours. Latterly there were fifteen journeys in each direction on this short shuttle between Audley End and Saffron Walden only (journey time four minutes). These included variations on Saturdays as well as seven through trains to Bartlow (journey time sixteen minutes), some of which then reversed to terminate at Haverhill on the Stour Valley line (journey time thirty-two minutes). There was also a limited Sunday service. Passenger trains were discontinued on 7 September 1964 and freight at the end of the year. Trains on the Stour Valley line served Bartlow until 1966.

This statuesque water column was still in situ at Haverhill on 23 November 1963.

Despite fierce opposition, the railways of Lincolnshire were decimated in the 1960s and early 1970s, leaving only the Sleaford-Boston-Skegness line on the eastern side of the county. One of the lines to succumb was the former GNR Lincolnshire Loop Line that linked Lincoln with Peterborough via Boston and which, for the first two years of its existence (1848-1850), was the main line from London to York. Stixwould, where this picture of a Derby-built heavyweight two-car DMU was taken on 8 March 1969, was served by trains that at this time only operated between Lincoln and Firsby on the 'New Line' via Woodhall Junction, until this closed on 5 October 1970, the line from Woodhall Junction to Boston having closed on 17 June 1963. The trackbed at Stixwould station, which is alongside the River Witham, is now the Water Rail Way footpath/cycleway, running between the platforms that are still in situ, together with a replica station nameboard. The stationmaster's red brick house behind the signal box is now joined to the signal box (concealed by the train) to create a single building that is a private residence and guest house/retreat home. Between the platform ends and the signal box is a small crossing that originally led to a chain ferry which crossed the river. DMUs were introduced on local services in the area in 1955.

The next station south of Stixwould was Woodhall Junction that, as evidenced in this view, was allowed to deteriorate, along with so many others in Lincolnshire, seemingly to deter passengers and facilitate closure. Like Stixwould, Woodhall Junction was located alongside the River Witham. It opened on 17 October 1848 as Kirkstead on the Lincolnshire Loop and became a junction when the Horncastle branch through Woodhall Spa opened on 11 August 1855. It became an even busier junction when the Kirkstead and Little Steeping Railway (the 'New Line') leading to Firsby opened in 1913. Indeed, with its extensive goods yard, Woodhall Junction at one time provided work for two dozen people. It was renamed in 1922 to capitalise on the increasing popularity of Woodhall Spa. The decline in the station's fortunes began when the Woodhall Spa/Horncastle branch closed to passengers on 13 September 1954, followed by the route to Boston on 17 June 1963 and finally the line to Firsby on 5 October 1970, which resulted in the closure of the station. Horncastle trains used a wrong-facing bay behind the up platform on the right requiring reversals. The Italianate style station house with its three-storey brick tower on the up platform, together with the booking hall, have been converted into a dwelling and several railway artefacts have been recreated by the owner who is a railway enthusiast.

Firsby was a busy junction with an imposing station building, complete with entrance colonnades and train shed roof. The station opened in 1848 on the East Lincolnshire Railway that linked Boston, Louth and Grimsby, with services operated by the GNR. Branches from here served Spilsby and Skegness, the latter line attracting vast numbers of holidaymakers who changed trains at Firsby. Passenger services to Spilsby were suspended on 11 September 1939 and never reinstated, and freight services ended on 30 November 1958. Train services still operate to Skegness via Boston but now turn off at Firsby South Junction, thereby avoiding Firsby station that closed on 5 October 1970 due to the abandonment of the line to Louth. The heritage Lincolnshire Wolds Railway, which operates a 1½ mile stretch of line southwards from its terminus at Ludborough, intends to reach Louth, but from the north. Blake took this view of Firsby station looking south on 22 June 1968. It shows a Derby-built two-car DMU at Platform 3 and the soon to be demolished pump house and water tower on the right. Part of the original station building survives as a private residence.

The following station northwards from Firsby towards Louth and the Mablethorpe Loop was Burgh-le-Marsh, seen here on 8 March 1969. Opened as Burgh by the East Lincolnshire Railway in 1848, it was renamed upon Grouping (the creation of the 'Big Four' railway companies) in 1923 to distinguish it from Burgh in Cumbria that was renamed Burgh-by-Sands about the same time. Until Skegness station opened in 1873, by which time this seaside resort was increasingly popular, holidaymakers would alight from their trains at Burgh-le-Marsh to be met by a horse-drawn omnibus to take them to 'Skeggy'. Freight services were withdrawn from Burgh-le-Marsh on 2 May 1966 and passenger services from 5 October 1970. The station site is relatively unchanged today in enthusiastic private hands, with the station house, waiting room, railwaymen's cottages and signal box all well preserved but the GNR somersault signal on its lattice post seen in the background has vanished. A GNR signal fitter, Edward French, designed this type of signal following an accident on the GNR in 1876 caused by the semaphore arm becoming frozen within the slot in the signal post. Somersault signals used a centrally balanced arm operated outside the signal post, ensuring the entire semaphore arm was always exposed.

Willoughby, the next station north from Burgh-le-Marsh, was a junction where the Mablethorpe Loop line to Louth split from the main line to Louth, the first station on the Loop being Mumby Road. Blake's photograph of this remote station, now appropriately replaced by farm buildings except for the Weigh Office that has been retained, perfectly illustrates the semi-derelict condition into which these East Lincolnshire lines had been allowed to fall. Combined with reductions in the availability of cheap tickets and a sparse timetable, every effort appears to have been made to discourage passengers and facilitate closure. On 5 December 1960, the 13 mile section from Louth to Mablethorpe closed but the 9¾ mile southern section from Mablethorpe to Willoughby, which included Mumby Road, survived until 5 October 1970. This was due initially to the volume of visitors from the south to the seaside resorts of Sutton-on-Sea and Mablethorpe, until the inevitable increase in private car ownership caused passenger numbers to dwindle excessively.

We now cross to Lancashire and to Manchester Victoria which, when it opened in 1844, was said to be the largest station in England. Forty years later traffic demand led to the Lancashire & Yorkshire Railway (L&Y) constructing a new station that, when rebuilt in 1903, became one of the biggest stations in Britain with seventeen platforms and an array of offices and other buildings. Trains operated by the LNWR had to run through Victoria to gain access to Manchester Exchange, its own adjacent station that opened in 1884. Platform 11, which linked the two stations, was the longest in Britain at 2,194ft. The L&Y was subsumed into the LNWR on 1 January 1922 and a year later, the LNWR became part of the newly created LMS. On 12 July 1963, Fairburn 2-6-4T, No.42180, with an old style (LMS) smoke box number plate, waits to depart.

Manchester Victoria had a mix of platforms where services departed for Scotland, the Lancashire heartlands, Blackpool, Liverpool and Southport as well as into Yorkshire. There were also heavily used local services to towns such as Blackburn, Bolton, Bury, Oldham and Rochdale, some of which are listed on the destination board in the upper photograph and on the delightful array of fingerboards in the lower view. These dated L&Y artefacts were still in use in July 1963 when these pictures were taken.

Today this station, Dane Road, is served by trams on the Manchester Metrolink line to Altrincham. Opened in 1931 when the Manchester, South Junction & Altrincham line was electrified, it survived as a four-platform station until closure by BR in December 1991 after which it was rebuilt before reopening as a Metrolink station in the following June. In this view one of the 1931 sets built by the Metropolitan Carriage and Wagon Company enters the station. When electrified, this was the first passenger line in England to work at 1,500 volts dc. Drawing power from a single pantograph, a three-car unit consisted of a driving motor with four 328hp motors and two trailers. In rush hours, sets could be coupled together to create six-car trains that often reached speeds of more than 60mph.

From 1870, the Bolton suburb of Horwich was served by a 1¼ mile branch off the Bolton-Chorley line. Traffic on this increased substantially following the opening in 1887 of the L&Y locomotive works, which was accessed directly from the branch. Steam locomotives were built at Horwich until 1957 after which the works handled various maintenance and repair work until final closure in the late 1980s. The handful of passenger services were mostly used by employees from the works with some trains having through carriages to and from Chorley, Bolton Trinity Street and Manchester Victoria. During the 1960s, enthusiasts visited Horwich to observe activity in and around the works and to ride on the steam-hauled push and pull service that took four minutes to travel between Horwich and Blackrod on the Bolton-Chorley line. On 17 July 1965, the normal steam train formation is on the right of the picture while a Cravens two-car DMU stands at the station platform. The passenger service closed on 25 September 1965 but goods traffic continued until April 1966 and the link into the works survived until 1989.

During his visit to the Bolton area on 17 July 1965, Blake also photographed Fairburn 2-6-4T, No.42132 (another one carrying an old-style smoke box number plate). It is entering Lostock Junction station, which was located at the point where the L&Y lines from Bolton to Preston and Wigan diverged. To cater for nearby industry, including an aircraft factory opened in the late 1930s, the original goods facilities were improved to include warehouses and a substantial array of sidings. After handling heavy tonnage during the Second World War, the goods yard closed in September 1963, the station in November 1966 and the last of the sidings in April 1967. On the credit side, a new Lostock station opened in 1988 on the Bolton-Preston line.

Many enthusiasts photographed DMUs at Gateacre, terminus of a local service from Liverpool Central that survived far longer than expected owing to problems over replacement buses. When the service finally closed in April 1972, most of the route was electrified and reopened less than six years later. However, the section between Hunts Cross and Gateacre was not included; the latter was the last station to remain open on the Cheshire Lines Committee (CLC) North Liverpool line, the first section of which had opened in 1879 with passenger trains eventually running to Aintree and Southport. Gateacre was unusual in being the only station on this line to have a subway connecting its two platforms. Furthermore, a walkway linked the down platform to the main station building over an area left clear for possible quadrupling. In its heyday the North Liverpool line handled considerable tonnage to and from the docks, excursion traffic to Southport and race traffic to Aintree. The line officially closed in February 1979 and is now a cycleway and footpath.

Liverpool was once served by the three mainline terminal stations fringing the central area, the last to open being Liverpool Central in 1874. Owing to the proximity of long-established buildings, the use of explosives had been forbidden so excavations were undertaken by hand. In this view a later-type Derby-built two-car DMU from Gateacre has just emerged from Great George Street tunnel and is approaching the end of its run. Right up to closure, the line enjoyed a good level of service and trains were well filled in rush hours.

Central had three island platforms, an attractive single span roof, a three-storey office block (former headquarters of the CLC) and from 1892 access to the Low Level station, terminus of the under-river Mersey Railway. For decades, fast trains to Manchester had departed from the High Level station but when this photograph was taken there was just a single operational platform. Following closure in 1972, this prime site was eventually cleared and is now occupied by Central Village. However, the much-altered Low Level is served by EMUs on Merseyrail's Northern Line.

While visiting some surviving steam outposts in north Lancashire, Blake photographed gas-lit Rose Grove station on 2 July 1968. Built 120 years earlier by the East Lancashire Railway it rapidly became an integral part of the expanding railway community with many employees living close to the station, loco shed and major interchange sidings, which at their height could handle up to 1,000 wagons. In the 1970s, the station buildings were demolished to be replaced by a much reduced facility that is served by trains on the East Lancashire line. Any of today's travellers unfamiliar with pre-decimal currency and seeing posters such as those shown here are probably wondering what a 'bob' is! It's a shilling in old money (now 5p).

Wennington was a rural junction in north-east Lancashire reached first in 1849 by the Midland Railway's Lune Valley line from Lancaster and then by the Furness & Midland Joint Railway from Carnforth in 1867. Wennington stopped being a junction following the withdrawal of freight services on the Lune Valley line on 8 January 1968, passenger services having ended on 3 January 1966. Today this stretch of line is still open, providing passenger services between Morecambe and Leeds/Bradford via Carnforth and Wennington. Having travelled along this route, Carnforth-based Fairburn 2-6-4T, No.42154 bursts out of the 1,230yd Melling Tunnel and passes the Wennington up distant signal on 9 October 1965. Wennington station was earmarked for closure by Beeching and, given the small community it serves, is fortunate to survive today. Melling station, on the other hand, closed as early as 1952 but the main building survives following conversion to residential use.

Blake's visit to the branch from Eryholme (formerly Dalton), south of Darlington, to Richmond (Yorks) on 15 February 1969, three weeks before closure, coincided with considerable snowfall in the area, making Richmond's distinctive station look even more Swiss than usual. The branch was intended to attract lucrative freight traffic from the lead mines in Swaledale but never reached that far, although the foreshortened line did carry freight and Richmond remained open for that purpose until 1967 when the sidings, including the two that occupied the left-hand side of the trainshed, were lifted. The line was opened in 1846 by the Yorkshire & Newcastle Railway (which was absorbed by the North Eastern Railway in 1854) and the station building seen here was completed in 1847. Passenger services to Richmond operated from Darlington and were due to be withdrawn in 1963 but because of strong objections the line struggled on until closure to passengers on 3 March 1969. Grade II listed, the station has been sympathetically converted into a leisure and retail centre called 'The Station'.

There were three intermediate stations on the Richmond branch (plus one on the mainline) including Scorton, also photographed on 15 February 1969 and featuring a Metro-Cammell DMU. The substantial station building is now a private residence.

The opening of Catterick Camp in 1916 brought considerable troop traffic to the Richmond branch and the Camp had its own military railway operated by the LNER following the Grouping of 1923. Regular passenger trains into the Camp were withdrawn from 26 October 1964 and Catterick Bridge station closed when passenger services on the Richmond branch finished from 3 March 1969, although it remained open for goods traffic until 9 February 1970.

On returning to Darlington after an exhausting few hours on the Richmond branch, Blake moved on to Bishop Auckland in Co Durham. His footprints are evidence that even by late afternoon on 15 February 1969 no one else had ventured to the western end of the platform that day to photograph the train shed and the DMU waiting to return to Darlington. This had once been a busy station with trains additionally going to Durham, Crook, Wearhead, Barnard Castle and Saltburn, on the East Coast. Much of the line followed the route of the famous Stockton & Darlington Railway, the world's first public railway to use steam traction that opened in 1825, albeit alongside horse power until 1833 when the railway became totally steam operated. Bishop Auckland station was triangular in design, with a curved platform for Durham trains out of the picture on the left. Although still open, the station now has just a single platform on the site of this one, the early twentieth century buildings being demolished in 1986. Today the station serves as a terminus for the 'Bishop Line' to Darlington and the 'Tees Valley Line' onwards to Saltburn. Part of the line west of Bishop Auckland to Stanhope is operated by the heritage Weardale Railway.

The Beeching Axe hovered over the Haltwhistle to Alston branch (1852) for several years before the thirteen mile line finally succumbed on 3 May 1976. Built mainly for the transportation of lead and coal it followed the course of the steeply sided South Tyne Valley. As it was under threat for so long, it became a natural target for photographers anxious to recapture the rural charm of so many doomed branches such as this one. On 17 April 1965, Blake took this scene at Haltwhistle with a Birmingham Railway Carriage & Wagon Co (BRCW) DMU in the platform. From here, trains climbed virtually all the way to Alston with a maximum grade of 1:56. For those in the know, train crews on the branch would sometimes make unofficial stops to allow passengers to clamber on and off at various points between stations.

On 18 April 1965 Blake composed this charming study of Lambley station. Located in the depths of the countryside, it featured a single platform, a substantial, two-storey Tudor-style stone building and elderly oil lamps. Until 1953, this was the starting point for a ten mile coal-carrying branch (the Brampton Railway) that began life in the mid-eighteenth century as a horse-drawn waggonway. Passenger services had been withdrawn by 1920 and the LNER closed the line in 1923, leasing it to the colliery owners. Access for trains going to and from Haltwhistle had involved reversing through the station. Just out of view on the right stands the magnificent nine-arch Lambley viaduct, now part of the South Tyne Trail that used to run past the privately owned station house but has since been diverted.

On 22 September 1963, when Blake travelled on the Metro-Cammell two-car DMU seen here, Alston station still had its train shed roof. The site included a single platform, a Tudor-style station building, an LNER nameboard, gas lamps, a loco shed (closed in 1959), a goods shed and an array of sidings that handled among other things livestock, ore, coal and lime. All goods traffic ended in September 1965. Although passenger traffic to this market town was always light, it was the unsuitability of the local roads to carry buses that kept the railway running for so long. At this time, there were six weekday departures from Alston with extras on Saturdays but no service on Sundays. The journey time was thirty-five minutes.

On returning to Alston on 17 April 1965, travelling on a BRCW two-car DMU, Blake discovered that the overall roof had been removed. Later, in January 1969, the station became unstaffed. With closure approaching, BR did try, belatedly, to promote the scenic nature of the line but to no avail. Following closure, attempts were made to establish a heritage operation but these came to nothing as BR had quickly lifted the track. However, since 1983, part of the branch has been home to a 2ft gauge line operated by the South Tynedale Railway whose headquarters are in the former station, now Grade II listed.

Determined to capitalise on the Victorian preoccupation with bracing outdoor activity, in June 1869 the Furness Railway opened a branch from Ulverston to the southern tip of Lake Windermere where passengers could transfer onto a railway-owned steamer for a sail to Bowness or Ambleside. As the southern Lakes became increasingly popular, through trains were operated from places like Morecambe and special sea, rail, lake and coach tours were introduced. When this traffic eventually declined, no passenger trains ran on the branch for some time. However, after the Second World War Windermere Lakeside Station reopened and, during the summer months, trains and through carriages arrived from Barrow, Morecambe, Blackpool and Preston until the 1960s. There were also special excursions. On 18 July 1965, 'Black Five' 4-6-0, No.44728 is waiting at Lakeside for passengers to disembark from one of the steamers and join the 'Lake Windermere Cruise' train.

Blake took several views of No.44728 on 18 July 1965 including its departure from Lakeside with the 'Lake Windermere Cruise' train en route for Morecambe. When this former Furness Railway line closed to passengers from 5 September 1965, it remained open for freight as far as Haverthwaite until April 1967. Then, after lying derelict for several years, the northern end was reopened in 1973 by the Lakeside & Haverthwaite Railway Company so once again people can change from train to steamer. Since 1984, the steamers have been in private ownership but the fleet includes several notable veterans: *Tern* (1891), *Teal* (1936) and *Swan* (1938). The heritage railway is home to the only two surviving Fairburn 2-6-4Ts, both Brighton-built.

As Windermere is classified as a public highway, vessels operating on the lake originally carried coal, timber, mail, farm produce and general merchandise as well as increasing numbers of tourists, especially day-trippers. Eventually railway warehouses opened at Ambleside and Bowness. In the 1870s, the Furness Railway took over the lake's steamer services with passengers transferring from rail to ship at the attractive Lakeside station, which in its heyday included an elegant assembly hall complete with restaurant, waiting rooms and baskets of hanging flowers. These facilities were located on the other side of the wall on the left of this photograph. Lakeside also had a goods yard, storage sidings and on the east side an area for ship repair and inspection work.

Located on the Cumbrian Coast line, Aspatria is one of the few stations depicted in this book that are still open today, although it is now an unstaffed halt. On a cold, frosty 21 December 1968, milk churns from a nearby cheese-making factory are being loaded onto an early Derby-built lightweight DMU. These were the first mass-produced units and were introduced in 1954, but due to being incompatible with other DMUs (hence the warning yellow diamond markings on the front), all were withdrawn from normal service by 1969. The station was opened as early as 1841 by the Maryport & Carlisle Railway (M&C) and was also the junction point until 1952 for the branch to Mealsgate. The last operational M&C signal box was located at Aspatria but was demolished in 1998.

Crossing the border into Scotland, the challenging seventy-four mile line from Dumfries to Stranraer, known by local railwaymen as 'The Port Road', which opened between 1859 and 1861, covered vast tracts of inhospitable and demanding terrain. For decades, the predominantly single track route was used by Anglo-Irish boat trains including the 'Northern Irishman', an overnight sleeper between Stranraer and London Euston, as well as by others conveying troops, cattle, coal and general merchandise. In addition to being an intermediate station on the Dunfries-Stranraer line, Castle Douglas, where this busy scene was captured on 19 April 1965, was also the junction for the Kirkcudbright branch that Standard Class 4 2-6-0, No.76073 is about to take. The reason why a Stanier 'Black 5' 4-6-0 is standing in front of the Standard 4 is unfortunately unknown.

Again on 19 April 1965, BR Standard Class 4 2-6-4T, No.80119 pauses at Castle Douglas en route to Dumfries while working one of the three weekday stopping trains still covering the whole route. Unlike others on the line, the station at Castle Douglas was convenient for the town but by the late 1950s trains were often virtually empty. Faced with closure, the men working 'The Port Road' offered to take lower wages but to no avail: the sparsely populated route serving scattered market communities closed to all traffic from 14 June 1965, after which Stranraer could only be reached by way of Mauchline and Ayr. Initially this line had also appeared in the Beeching Report but following pressure from, among others, the Northern Ireland government, it was reprieved.

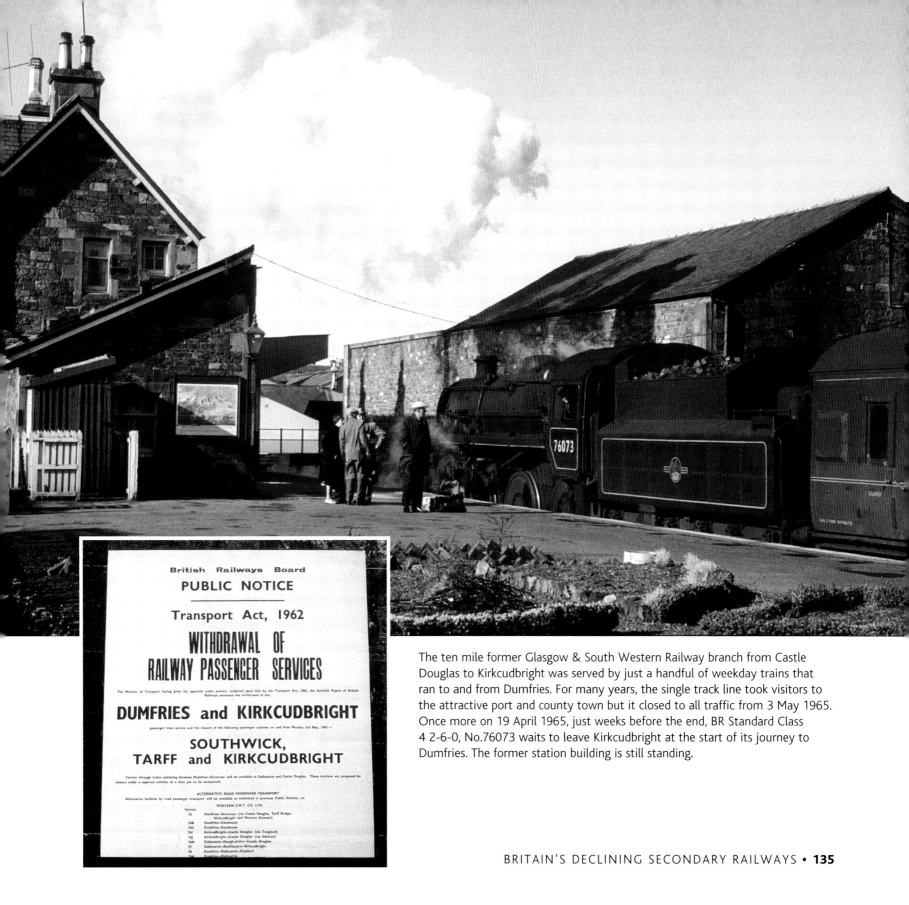

The ten mile former Glasgow & South Western Railway branch from Castle Douglas to Kirkcudbright was served by just a handful of weekday trains that ran to and from Dumfries. For many years, the single track line took visitors to the attractive port and county town but it closed to all traffic from 3 May 1965. Once more on 19 April 1965, just weeks before the end, BR Standard Class 4 2-6-0, No.76073 waits to leave Kirkcudbright at the start of its journey to Dumfries. The former station building is still standing.

The small Scottish town of Langholm was served from 1864 by a short, seven mile branch from Riddings Junction on the mainline from Carlisle to Edinburgh (the Waverley route). Goods traffic was generated by local mills and by the movement of agricultural and domestic produce. Although passenger traffic was never substantial, the branch allowed local residents to reach Carlisle or to go north towards Edinburgh. Excursions also ran to Murrayfield for rugby internationals and to Silloth for recreational purposes. For a while, some passenger duties were operated by steam railcars but otherwise the branch, with its two intermediate stations, was worked by steam until closed for passengers from 15 June 1964. Freight traffic was not withdrawn until 18 September 1967. Latterly Ivatt Class 4 2-6-0s ('Flying Pigs') based at Carlisle Kingmoor mpd were regular performers and one of these, No.43103, simmers at the single platform station before leaving for Carlisle on 23 September 1963. The engine shed closed in 1932 but remained in place, without roof or track, until the end as one side acted as the platform wall and had previously supported the original train shed roof.

Some ten miles east of Langholm was Kershopefoot station on the English section of the Waverley route. This view of the nameboard was taken in December 1968 shortly before the ninety-eight mile cross-border line closed amid much controversy on 5 January 1969, albeit now partly reinstated.

As with so many branch lines, traffic on the Langholm branch had dwindled dramatically during the 1950s, so that in the final years the thirty-two weekday trains only carried 350 passengers. After offloading, arriving trains reversed so the loco could run round before coupling up and propelling the carriages back into the platform, an earlier turntable having long since disappeared. Latterly staff at many stations had ample time to keep their stations spotless and, in this instance, to also create attractive floral displays. This whole site including the goods yard was cleared for redevelopment in 1970.

Connecting with the Waverley route at St Boswells was another long rural railway that started at Tweedmouth and during its thirty-three miles served a string of isolated, low-density communities. Opened in stages between 1849 and 1851, with the North Eastern Railway advancing westwards to Kelso and the North British Railway proceeding eastwards to Kelso, this joined-up cross-border route closed to passengers from 15 June 1964. Some sections survived for freight, the last being Kelso to St Boswells that closed in March 1968. Passenger trains remained steam-hauled to the end. On 25 September 1963, after an overnight stay at St Boswells, Blake boarded the 8.25am departure to Berwick, one of only two through weekday trains, which was hauled tender-first by No.78047, a BR Standard Class 2 2-6-0 from Hawick mpd. Here it is seen at Kelso, alongside a resplendent, lined-out LMS (Stanier) full brake (BG), contrasting with the unlined BR BG on the right. The journey time in both directions was about ninety minutes and involved reversals at Tweedmouth.

On the return working, No.78047 was smoke box first when photographed at Coldstream, the junction for the former line to Alnwick of which the section to Wooler carried freight until 1965. Coldstream was one of only two stations still open between Tweedmouth and Kelso, the rest having closed in 1955. However, nothing was done to improve overall timings and the slow pace allowed for any shunting and delays at passing loops; it also gave visiting enthusiasts time to take their photographs. Occasionally engineering work meant trains off the East Coast mainline had been diverted over this sleepy backwater.

Blake's next photograph on his epic round trip was taken at Roxburgh, junction for the branch to Jedburgh (closed to passengers in August 1948 and goods in August 1964). No 78047 stands opposite a sister engine on the Jedburgh goods. For much of their life, revenue on these isolated lines came from the movement of livestock but with the transfer to lorries such sparsely used links were no longer financially viable. However, for those without access to cars or buses, these services were vital lifelines especially during harsh winter months when roads were often blocked by snowdrifts. By the late 1950s, loadings were so light that a single coach sufficed.

The final picture on this straggling cross-country line was taken at Rutherford, the penultimate station before St Boswells. It gives a good view of the single coach, a 63ft brake composite corridor coach (BCK) of LNER Thompson design, with distinctive oval toilet windows. Such coaches were built from 1945-1951 for express services until superseded by the new BR Standard Mark I stock. Thompson became the LNER's Chief Mechanical Engineer following Gresley's sudden death in 1941 and, on retirement in 1946, was succeeded by Peppercorn. Although there are no signs of any passengers alighting or boarding at Rutherford, the train is by no means empty.

The caption on page 139 refers to the railway from Coldstream to Alnwick. Opened by the North Eastern Railway in 1887, this thirty-six mile line closed to passengers in 1930 but Alnwick remained connected to the railway system until closure in 1968, being served by through trains from Newcastle and Berwick and a shuttle service from Alnmouth. Opening in 1850, DMUs took over the shuttle from June 1966, replacing the Peppercorn K1 Class 2-6-0s that latterly provided the regular motive power. North British-built K1, No.62021, built in 1949, is seen on the 2¾ mile branch on 16 October 1965. The Aln Valley Railway Trust has started work on reopening the line.

Sometimes it was hard to understand why certain rail services survived as long as they did. One such was the single weekday journey along the full length of the three mile branch from Arkleston Junction to Renfrew Wharf – a line with an interesting history. Opened in 1837 to serve the growing Clyde-based industries, the 4ft 6in gauge line was operated by steam locos until 1842 and then by horses. In 1866, it was re-gauged, doubled throughout, converted to steam haulage and linked to the main Glasgow & Paisley Joint Railway at Arkleston Junction. For many years, it had carried heavy workmen's traffic to nearby shipyards but, latterly, Renfrew Wharf exuded an air of neglect even though, as seen here on 5 July 1966, the line survived into the diesel era, illustrated here by a Metro-Cammell three-car DMU.

On 5 July 1966, Blake had risen early to catch the 7.18am DMU from Glasgow St Enoch, which some forty minutes later terminated among the weeds at Renfrew Wharf. There was little sign of life at the station apart from a 'gentleman of the road' (or should that be 'railway'?) whose slumbers were disturbed by the train. Although the sun failed to shine, Blake broke his usual rule to record this decrepit location with its overgrown track and absence of station buildings. This single weekday journey survived until 5 June 1967. The short section from Arkleston Junction to Sandyford remained open for goods until 1981, the line north of South Renfrew having closed completely in 1978.

On 24 September 1963, Blake made a special trip to photograph the railbuses assigned to the fifteen mile Gleneagles to Comrie service, only to find steam had been substituted. When introduced in 1958 it was hoped the railbuses would give the line a new lease of life. Some new halts were also opened between Gleneagles and Crieff. However, the railbuses proved unreliable, being prone to frequent mechanical failure. Traversing relatively flat farmland, the service incorporated some of a former line to Balquhidder, parts of which had only opened in 1905. Here, 'Black 5' No.44999 is seen at Crieff in charge of the one-coach train. Originally named The Terminus, this station opened in 1856: it had two platforms and a through centre road. As Crieff had formerly been a busy junction there was a loco shed and an extensive goods yard. By the time of Blake's visit, the once-elegant station was in disrepair. Passenger traffic ended on 6 July 1964 but freight continued on the Almond Valley line to Perth until 1967. The whole site was subsequently cleared.

After closure of the unprofitable section west to Balquhidder in 1959, a headshunt was built at Comrie. However, following introduction of the railbuses in 1958 only the westbound platform was used, this arrangement continuing until closure. On 24 September 1963, the driver of No.44999 chats to a couple of enthusiasts before returning to Gleneagles. The first passenger train to Comrie arrived on 1 July 1893. The last one departed on 4 July 1964 hauled by Standard Class 4 2-6-4T, No.80063.

The former Caledonian & Oban line from Dunblane to Crianlarich (1870) and the associated five mile branch from Killin Junction to Loch Tay (1886) were listed for closure in the Beeching Report. Both were financed by local landowners and eventually became part of the Caledonian Railway. During the holiday season, thousands of visitors used these lines with many boarding the steamer, *Lady of the Lake*, at Loch Tay. However, when war was declared in September 1939, the Killin-Loch Tay section lost its passenger service, although it remained open for goods and for access to a small loco shed where engines were coaled directly from mineral wagons. In the 1950s, the branch transported materials for the construction of new dams. Killin station was spartan with wooden buildings, a single platform and a few sidings on the west side. Latterly there were five weekday trips in each direction taking between thirteen and fourteen minutes. Here BR Standard Class 4 2-6-4T, No.80093 waits to tackle the steep grades up to the junction on 25 September 1963. Although long associated with steam, diesel locos did occasionally appear on goods trains, and DMUs were employed on 'The Six Lochs Landcruise'. A landslip at Glen Ogle led to the premature closure of the branch and the 'mainline' on 27 September 1965.

Another line with a sparse passenger service was that from Connel Ferry to Ballachulish (1903). This twenty-seven mile branch was built to bring slate from Ballachulish down to the mainline. The local quarries, which closed in 1955, had their own internal narrow gauge railways with a connection to the goods yard on the north side of the two-platform station that was re-named Ballachulish (Glencoe) for Kinlochleven in 1908. As late as the 1950s there had been plans to construct an extension north from Ballachulish towards Fort William to avoid the circuitous West Highland line. However, when this came to nothing, freight traffic ended in June 1965 and passenger traffic on 28 March 1966, two days after Blake made his photographic pilgrimage. The limited passenger service consisted of three weekday trains in each direction plus an extra on Saturdays. Latterly these were operated by diesel locos such as this BRCW Type 2. Today the site is occupied by houses and a medical centre.

The Beeching cuts virtually wiped out the rail network in north-east Scotland. The decimation could have been worse if the lines from Inverness to Thurso, Wick and the Kyle of Lochalsh had not been reprieved. During the 1960s, Blake made several trips to cover the threatened lines. On 13 March 1965 he spent time at Maud Junction (called at different times Banks, Brucklay and Maud) that, despite the sparsity of the service, boasted four platforms, tea rooms and a buffet. It was here that the line from Dyce split – one prong going east to Peterhead and the other north to Fraserburgh. Both were major fishing ports and over the years millions of tonnes of fresh fish would pass through Maud Junction en route to London in special refrigerated containers. The Junction was also the regional railhead for the bulk movement of cattle. However, it had relatively few sidings and no loco shed, although it did have a turntable. From 1959 until closure on 4 October 1965, passenger services were dieselised, as illustrated here by three of the unsuccessful North British (NBL) Type 2 locomotives, two apparently being needed to haul three Stanier coaches! Freight services continued for another fourteen years and included the delivery of massive pipes for the North Sea oil industry. Today one part of the former station buildings houses the Maud Railway Museum.

The thirty-eight mile line from Dyce to Peterhead opened in stages during 1861-62 with a further extension to Peterhead harbour following in 1865. From 1866, the lines in this area were taken over by the Great North of Scotland Railway (GNS). This view of Peterhead Station depicting an NBL Type 2 diesel locomotive was taken on 28 January 1964 The train shed (overall roof) covered only one of the two passenger platforms. The goods line on the right had a seperate platform behind the photographer. The passenger service to Maud Junction ended on 3 May 1965, although freight used the line until September 1970.

The sixteen mile section north from Maud Junction to Fraserburgh opened in 1865. The main source of revenue was fish, coal, livestock and agricultural produce. After 1948, Dyce-Fraserburgh became the mainline with Peterhead reduced to branch status. The terminal facilities included a loco shed, extensive sidings and a three-platform station under a glazed roof. In this view taken on 28 January 1964, a BRCW Type 2 diesel locomotive stands outside the two-road loco shed; an NBL Type 2 is at the head of a train to Aberdeen, and the Cravens DMU on the right is working the St Combs Light Railway. Latterly there were five return trips to Aberdeen on Mondays to Saturdays with a journey time of about ninety minutes. Although passenger services ended on 4 October 1965, freight continued until October 1979. At the height of the boom in North Sea oil there was talk of reopening the line and today consideration is being given to re-instating the lines to both Fraserburgh and Peterhead.

One of the most unusual lines in this area was the St Combs Light Railway, which crossed flat, open country close to the sea. Opened by the GNS in July 1903, there was a speed restriction of 25mph and as the light railway was largely unfenced the steam locomotives were equipped with cow-catchers. When Blake rode the five mile line on 28 January 1964 the turn round at St Combs was so rapid he only just had time to take this photograph. The site of the former run round loop can be seen on the left. Even towards the end, there were eleven return journeys, most trains being well used. Cost-cutting measures had included the introduction of DMUs, the closure of the loss-making goods service and removal of staff from all the branch stations. However, all this failed to save the line and it was abandoned on 3 May 1965. The site of the former station is now occupied by houses.

A group of lines serving the Banff and Moray coast were closed between 1964 and 1968. These included the branch from Tillynaught to the fishing port of Banff, which had been opened in 1859 as part of a steeply graded route from a junction at Grange on the main line from Aberdeen to Keith. From 1863, these lines were operated by the GNS and following completion in 1866 of the Company's alternative Aberdeen to Elgin route by way of the Moray coast, Banff was reduced to branch status with connections to and from Tillynaught. The six mile line had four intermediate stations including three halts. The facilities at Banff included a goods yard, a small loco shed with coaling and water facilities, and a covered terminal building for passengers. Latterly BR Standard Class 2 2-6-0, No.78045 worked most trains and is seen here on 25 January 1964 waiting to depart for Tillynaught. On 4 July 1964, this same loco worked the final passenger duty, with goods traffic ending four years later in May 1968.

Keith is one of the few stations in this part of north-east Scotland that is still open. In the past, the GNS and Highland Railway (HR) routes from Inverness and Aberdeen converged here and, for many years, it was known as Keith Junction. Eventually there were four platforms, two east-facing bays, extensive sidings and an associated loco shed. Following closure of the passenger service to Elgin via Craigellachie on 6 May 1968, the track layout was rationalised in the 1970s and the station now has a single platform for both directions plus a bay for emergencies. Freight to Elgin via Craigellachie continued until November 1968 and to Aberlour on the Speyside line until November 1971. Freight movements to the distillery at Dufftown continued for many more years and this section of track was also used by luxury excursion trains taking visitors to the distillery. Today this same section is home to the heritage Keith & Dufftown Railway, which is marketed as 'The Whisky Line'. On 15 March 1965, M79972, one of five fifty-seater Park Royal railbuses dating from 1958, was working the 9.40am to Aviemore via Craigellachie. All of these railbuses were gone by 1968 and none has been preserved.

Listed for closure by Beeching, the thirty-three miles from Craigellachie to Boat of Garten was memorable. Opened between 1863 and 1866, the single track 'Speyside' line followed the course of the river. Revenue came from the local whisky industry with train loads of coal, barley and wooden casks destined for distilleries located close to the line. Many tales surrounded the methods used to illegally extract whisky from the trains leaving the distilleries. Other commodities included timber and general goods. To reduce costs and attract new passengers, diesel railbuses were introduced in 1958 and four new halts were opened. During his photographic expedition on 15 March 1965, Blake encountered open hostility from the guard (soon to be made redundant) but undeterred he took this atmospheric view of M79972 at Knockando (formerly Dalbeallie) at 10.36am, with the signalman handing over the token. Knockando was one of several passing places, another being Ballindalloch (see lamp). Each railbus carried a small flight of steps to help passengers on and off. Latterly the service comprised three workings each way Monday to Friday with an extra round trip on Saturday evenings. Loadings were light, journey time was a leisurely seventy minutes and the loss-making service ended on 18 October 1965 with goods traffic remaining as far as Aberlour until November 1971. Today this station and its signal box still survive. Now renamed Tamdhu, it was for a while a visitor centre for the adjacent distillery of the same name on whose land it stands.

The 12.25pm return trip from Aviemore on 15 March 1965 was loco-hauled by a Derby-built Sulzer Type 2 diesel locomotive as the railbus had failed. At Craigellachie connections were made with routes to Elgin and Keith. These lines, which opened in the 1860s, also derived the bulk of their revenue from whisky. When the twenty-seven mile section from Elgin to Keith via Craigellachie closed to passengers on 6 May 1968 it virtually wiped out the rail network north of Aberdeen except for the service to Inverness via Elgin along the former HR from Keith. In its heyday, Craigellachie had been a busy junction handling a mix of goods, but mostly materials for the whisky distilleries. Today it is a car park. Blake took this view of Craigellachie station and trespass notice on 15 March 1965. He ended this particular trip by returning to Euston 'on the cushions'.

It is June 1969 and this is Brora station, looking north, on ScotRail's 'Far North Line', which is served by trains operating between Inverness and Wick/Thurso. The station building, dating from 1895, is boarded up at the moment, with proposals for non-railway use having so far failed. The line between Golspie and West Helmsdale passing through Brora was built by the Duke of Sutherland to serve his estate at Dunrobin. The Duke ran the line from its opening on 1 November 1870 until 14 June 1871 when the HR took over its operation, eventually owning it in 1884. The next station south of Brora, Dunrobin Castle, is unusual because, although managed by ScotRail, it is privately owned (by the Sutherland family) and is not normally served by trains during the winter when the Castle is closed. The Duke's own 0-4-4T locomotive, *Dunrobin*, and one of his saloons have recently been repatriated from Canada following purchase by the Beamish Museum in Co Durham.

Thurso is Great Britain's northernmost station and was opened by the HR in 1874. It is served by trains from Inverness, 154 miles and nearly four hours away. In the days of locomotive haulage, passenger trains consisted of two portions, one destined for Thurso and the other for Wick, the train being divided at Georgemas Junction, where a second engine waited. With the introduction of multiple units, the same train can now serve both termini, returning to Georgemas Junction station each time before finally departing for Inverness. In this view dating from 22 February 1969 depicting the movement of mail, there is something strange about the formation of the train because next to the coach stands an unfitted six-tonne wagon (distinguishable by being painted grey rather than reddish-brown 'bauxite') that should not be attached to a passenger train. Perhaps a shunting operation is taking place.

This photograph of Wick taken in June 1969 belies the fact that this was once a significant terminus with a busy goods yard and, out of view on the right, a two-road engine shed with a turntable. The line was built by the Sutherland & Caithness Railway in 1874, joining Wick and Thurso to the Duke of Sutherland's Railway at Helmsdale. Wick was also the terminus of the Wick and Lybster Light Railway that operated from 1903 to 1944. As mentioned on the previous page, Wick is served by trains from Inverness but the diversion to Thurso extends journey times to more than four hours. As with Thurso, the train shed roof is still intact but much of the remaining railway site has been developed, although the engine shed survives, albeit not visibly, having been incorporated within a supermarket.

With a sister living in Lurgan, Blake made frequent trips to Northern Ireland. On 6 November 1965 he visited the former Great Northern Railway (Ireland) (GNRI) Adelaide engine shed at Belfast, which was built in 1911. The GNRI, formed in 1876, became a cross-border railway operator when Ireland was partitioned in 1921 and was nationalised by both governments in 1953 who then jointly ran the railway. In May 1958, the assets and lines were divided between the two jurisdictions. This photograph depicts, apart from piles of neatly numbered railway sleepers, ex-GNRI Class UG 0-6-0, No.149, now renumbered Ulster Transport Authority (UTA) No.49. This locomotive, seen shunting wagons still bearing the initials GN, was built by Beyer, Peacock in 1948 and fitted with a Stanier-style tender. No.49 was the last of its class to remain in service and was broken up at Adelaide depot in 1970. The nine-road shed has since been demolished and replaced by a new train maintenance facility for Northern Ireland Railways. Guests attending the opening ceremony on 12 December 2012 arrived on a vintage train hauled by 1879-built Class J15, No.186.

Ordered by the Northern Counties Committee (NCC), a class WT 2-6-4T makes a spirited departure from Portadown on 4 January 1965. The NCC was formed in 1903 and belonged to the Midland Railway and, upon Grouping in Great Britain in 1923, to the newly created London, Midland and Scottish Railway (LMS). Shortly after mainland nationalisation in 1948, the NCC transferred to the newly formed UTA. The influence of the LMS naturally pervaded the NCC, as evidenced by the tender on page 160, and by the locomotive pictured here. Eighteen WT tanks, nicknamed 'Jeeps', were built between 1946 and 1950 at Derby, somewhat resembling Fowler's pre-war design of 2-6-4T and were numbered 1-10 and 50-57. Steam haulage of normal passenger and freight trains ended in May 1970 but a few were retained until October 1970 working stone trains in connection with a land reclamation scheme for a new motorway. One (No.4) has been preserved by the Railway Preservation Society of Ireland (RPSI).

Venturing south of the Irish border, Blake sampled the Loughrea branch where he photographed CIE Class 201, No.C201 preparing to leave Attymon Junction, Co Galway, on 4 November 1968, with a mixed train. Attymon station, situated on the Dublin-Galway main line, remains open today but the former station building, on the extreme left of the photograph, is now boarded up and used as a track maintenance store. The locomotive was the first of thirty-four such diesel electrics built by Metropolitan-Vickers of Manchester in 1956-57 and designed for branch line work. However, branch closures in the 1960s meant finding different duties for the class, for which they were underpowered. Consequently, all were subsequently fitted with larger engines, whereupon their number prefixes were changed from C to B. C201 became B201 and was the first-class member withdrawn following bomb damage in 1973.

The nine mile Midland Great Western Railway branch from Attymon Junction to Loughrea opened on 1 December 1890 and had one intermediate station, Dunsandle. Passenger numbers held up for some time, as illustrated in this picture taken on 4 November 1968 at Loughrea, with the line outliving many other rural branches. However, passenger services eventually ended on 1 November 1975, with sugar beet traffic ceasing soon after. A preservation scheme failed and the track was lifted in 1988. The station buildings seen here are derelict at the moment but still intact and the water tower, out of view, is incorporated into a modern industrial unit, with a small section visible.

A typical branch line cattle train is pictured at Limerick on 26 August 1962 headed by Great Southern & Western Railway (GS&WR) Class 101 (later Class J15) 0-6-0, No.190. This type was the most numerous class of locomotive in Ireland, 111 being constructed between 1866 and 1903. Testament to their success was their longevity, with an average operational life of seventy-five years. The locomotives were designed by Beyer, Peacock of Manchester under the direction of the GS&WR's Locomotive Engineer, Alexander McDonnell, who was in post from 1864 until he left for the North Eastern Railway in 1882. Many J15s were rebuilt with large superheated boilers and Belpaire fireboxes but No.190, dating from 1881, still carries an early boiler with round topped firebox, although it has lost its original outside-sprung tender in favour of a larger type. Two members of the class have been preserved by the RPSI: No.184 with original-style boiler and No.186, a rebuilt example.

Kilfree Junction, Co Sligo, was a station on the Dublin to Sligo main line between Boyle and Collooney. This photograph taken on 17 August 1962 depicts Class J18 0-6-0, No.574 on the branch train to Ballaghaderreen, Co Roscommon. This 9¾ mile line, with intermediate stations at Island Road and Edmondstown, opened on 2 November 1874 and closed on 4 February 1963. The locomotive was built by the Midland Great Western Railway (MGWR) in 1891 as No.80 *Dunsandle* and became No.574 in 1925 following absorption of the MGWR into the Great Southern Railway. It was withdrawn in 1963 after hauling the last passenger train from Ballaghaderreen on 2 February 1963. There is no trace of Kilfree Junction today apart from a section of the island platform and the stationmaster's house that, much altered, is now a private residence, and just a single track passes through the site.

The stock for the Ballaghaderreen branch train stands at the terminus. Traffic was mainly agricultural, transportation of cattle being particularly important, whereas passenger traffic was relatively sparse, with only three trains a day. A latterday curiosity of the line was the daily arrival of a crow that would hitch a ride perched on the coal in the tender (maybe it was fed by the footplate crew!). Since closure, the station building at Ballaghaderreen has fallen into disrepair but its remains still stand. Part of the platforms also survive and the goods shed has been converted into St Nathy's parish hall, but the small engine shed and water tower have been demolished and a health centre now stands on the site. The railway track in the foreground accentuates the difference in width between the Irish gauge of 5ft 3ins and the standard gauge in Great Britain of 4ft 8½ins.

In latter years, activity at Ballaghaderreen station revolved around the Plunkett family. During his visit to the station on 17 August 1962, Blake took this wonderful portrait of Christie Plunkett, the branch train guard, whose wife, Annie, issued tickets, operated the level crossing gates and acted as signalman. There was no separate signal box, the apparatus being housed in the station building. In 2010, the children of St Aidan's National School, Monasteraden, Co Sligo, compiled a film about the branch that included archive footage of the last day of service and interviews with people such as Leo Plunkett whose father features prominently in the old sequences.

Index

Station Page